# SAVING
# RUGBY UNION

To Rory Gillen, for making the publication of
*Saving Rugby Union* a reality.

"Somebody is going to have to try very hard to convince me
that we produce superior footballers today. Bigger ones, no doubt.
And fitter. And a heck of a lot richer.

"For me, alas, there has been too much change that has
been made with too much haste. Rugby never did need much
improving and I'll say farewell with one final thought.
Why would anyone want to mess with Mozart?"

**Welshman Michael Blair's farewell to rugby in the professional
era published on 3 September 2005 after ending his 40-year
career covering the game for *The Birmingham Post*.**

# SAVING
# RUGBY UNION
## THE PRICE OF PROFESSIONALISM

# ROSS REYBURN

*y* olfa

ISBN: 978-1-912631-32-2

Published and printed in Wales
on paper from well-maintained forests by
Y Lolfa Cyf., Talybont, Ceredigion SY24 5HE
*website* www.ylolfa.com
*e-mail* ylolfa@ylolfa.com
*tel* 01970 832 304
*fax* 832 782

Rugby union in the modern professional era became more popular but also more dangerous than ever. On the 25th anniversary of the game turning professional, Ross Reyburn examined the damaging mismanagement of the sport since the 1995 decision to pay players.

# FOREWORD

# "Why did they change our game?"

By Willie John McBride CBE, MBE,
former Ireland and British & Irish Lions captain

RUGBY TODAY IS nothing like the game I played.

It is a mixture of rugby union and rugby league – which is a huge influence on rugby union, with players lined up across the field against each other – and American football, with the obstruction and blocking.

In the modern game you can theoretically keep the ball for 40 minutes with endless phases. In the amateur era, once you went to ground you had to release the ball and get away. Players then could drive over the ball rucking the ball.

Today, when guys go to ground they still hold onto the ball and actually place it back with their hands. The referees allow that. It enables sides to retain the ball for phase after phase as it is so difficult for defenders to get hold of the ball at the breakdown. It's absolutely ridiculous.

There were never any serious injuries in rucks because you really had to release the ball and get away to avoid being raked back. If you held onto the ball you would be penalised. Today there are more and more pile-ups with knees and elbows hitting other players, causing injuries. Referees blow up for a scrum when the ball is buried in a pile of bodies. This simply wouldn't happen in a ruck situation when I played.

At the breakdown, I just don't understand why people are tackling players who haven't got the ball. It's not sport – they are just charging into people to take them out. Surely the law says you cannot tackle a player who hasn't got the ball? Obstruction offences are also continually ignored. Players run into the line of opponents chasing kicks and players being lifted to receive kick-offs invariably have a couple of their teammates in front of them, getting in the way of opponents trying to reach the ball.

In my day, Ireland were always short of outstanding players. But one thing we could always do was scrummage. We normally had a good scrummage against anybody in the world. Our prop forward Ray McLoughlin was a great technician. Another guy who was brilliant was our hooker Ken Kennedy. He was a contortionist. He would get in all sorts of body positions to win the ball.

In the modern era, referees have ignored the law by allowing the crooked scrum feed, ending the art of hooking. It has been a farce. Today scrum-halves practically feed the ball as if it is going into a rugby league scrum. It goes, more or less, into the second row.

There is an injuries crisis in rugby. You look at every international game that is played. How many do you see that are injury-free? I believe every player should be playing for 80 minutes unless he has to leave the field injured. I played for 14 years and never left the field in my life.

I've seen young guys from academies who have been told: "You are too light. You have got to put on two stones if you are to be successful." Kids are growing. They are fed on all these food supplements I call drugs and doing all these weights. Their bones can't take what their muscles are demanding. This is wrong. The one thing I was taught when I was growing up was to be supple. They are muscle-bound and more prone to injuries.

I was lucky I was brought up on a farm. I was naturally

strong. I remember being told, "when you go to ground, be supple like a rag doll and they'll kick you all day and never hurt you". It's a stupid thing to say but it was right.

It is terrible seeing all these people running off and on the pitch in an international. Recently a player was brought on with a minute to go – it could make no difference to the result. I once asked my old adversary Colin Meads how would you feel if they took you off with 20 minutes to go? I can't repeat what he said, but it was more or less 'you can stuff the game'.

I also find it disturbing the ease with which players can just switch their national allegiance. It devalues international rugby. When Wales defeated Ireland 25–7 in Cardiff in the 2019 Six Nations tournament, all the Welsh points were scored by two New Zealanders, Gareth Anscombe and Hadleigh Parkes. That can't be right. If you play for Ireland, you should have Irish blood coursing through your veins. The residential qualification should be ten years and that would end players playing for a country when they have no immediate family connection.

The one thing the Irish Rugby Union got right is that they own the players. England were stupid, as the RFU allowed the Premiership clubs to take control of the players. That has killed the Lions tour, which is very close to my heart and was a very big part of my rugby life. In the amateur days, we were people from all walks of life. It was a great exercise in humanity.

I find it very sad. The Lions tour is absolutely unique. There is no other sport that takes the best players from four countries on a tour abroad every four years – it is revered in New Zealand, South Africa and Australia, where the players are looked upon as heroes.

There were things you are told in life you never forget. When I joined Ballymena Rugby Club in 1958, I always remember a man called Paddy Owens, who was the club chairman, pointing to the entrance of the club and telling me: "That gate is open to everyone, all fellows, all creeds, provided you accept our principles and standards. We teach young men to be tolerant and understanding of their fellow beings. We also teach them how to be successful and more important, how to cope with disappointment. That is why we play rugby football."

These were lessons for life, not just rugby football. That is why I was annoyed when I saw the English players in the World Cup in Japan with the attitude 'we have got the wrong medal' when they were handed losers medals after South Africa won the final. Have we lost our ability to cope with losing?

The game today is all about money. The amateur game is certainly dying in my province, Ulster. I can't speak for elsewhere, but Colin Meads told me you now see soccer posts on school grounds everywhere in New Zealand.

I was so lucky to play in my era with so many great players. A few days before he died, Jackie Kyle, the great Irish fly-half in the post-war era, told me: "I don't understand why players run into each other. When I was playing, I used to run away from players!"

Any game is all about space. The modern game is all about closing down space with players lining across the field because of phase rugby.

The one thing that strikes me is why did they change our game?

Ballyclare, Northern Ireland
February 2020

# But what if they were right?

IN THE FIRST *25 years of the professional era, journalists, famous former internationals, coaches, medical experts and some current players highlighted the worrying problems within rugby union. What follows are examples of the many ignored calls for change and World Rugby's contrasting views on the state of the sport.*

"The changes in the tackle law were made to speed up play. They have not succeeded. Instead they have introduced the pile-up, as players seek to keep the ball off the ground and opponents seek to smother it. They have devalued the tackle and they have almost eliminated the ruck."

**The great Welsh coach Carwyn James**
**and *Daily Telegraph* correspondent John Reason**
**in their book *The World of Rugby* published in 1979.**

"This new midfield 'crash-ball' is a disaster – hunks of manhood with madness in their eyes, battering-ram bulldozers happy to be picked off on the gain-line by just-as-large hunks from the opposing side. For what? Just to do it all over again."

**Carwyn James in his *Guardian***
**newspaper column before his death in 1983.**

"Rugby league from its earliest days has been an alliance of heavy-contact brute force and terrific athleticism, and good luck to it. Fair enough. But rugby union boasted different priorities. Not anymore. Full-time pro rugby means full-time pro-weightlifters, I am told they are at it noon and night from Harlequins to Hartlepool."

**The late Frank Keating in his**
***Guardian* column, 10 September 1998.**

"Instead of being a means of restarting the game, it has become a way of winning penalties. To be frank, the whole edifice has become a grotesque farce and is blighting the game. Not only has the scrum become tedious, but it is dangerous. Ironically, the solution is the simple application of the existing laws."

**Former England hooker**
**Brian Moore, March 2013.**

"It was a sport for all shapes and sizes, then it became a sport for freaks. There is an inevitability that serious injuries will continue to rise. The human body is not meant to take that amount of force."

**Leading orthopaedic surgeon Professor John Fairclough,**
**interviewed by *The Rugby Paper*, 25 November 2013.**

"If it's all going to be about size, then rugby union will die. The players now are much bigger, less skilful and it's all about power now. Before any game the players are warming up for an hour and a half, that is totally ridiculous. It's all because of these fitness coaches who feel they need to justify their jobs."

**The great Welsh full-back JPR Williams,**
**an orthopaedic surgeon, 29 November 2013.**

"The breakdown is a pretty ugly place when you've got three 18-stoners flying in, trying to take your head off. Sometimes I'm struggling to shampoo my head the next day because my head is hurting so bad."

**Wales and British & Irish Lions
captain Sam Warburton, November 2014.**

"Modern rugby has developed to the point where if it goes down any more avenues it will cease to be rugby and become another game. We are getting very close to American football with all the delays, the TMO, multiple officials, the use of technology, huge numbers of replacements seemingly coming and going at will."

**Writer Michael Green, author of
*The Art of Coarse Rugby*, speaking in December 2014.**

"Some key laws appear to have fallen into complete disuse, with wholesale sections of the rule book containing what amounts to ghost law.

"This season, World Rugby stamped its feet. Well, more like shuffled them. It declared that the ball should be fed in straight at the scrum down the middle of the tunnel formed by the two front rows ... For about two weeks, referees complied and occasionally (the daredevils) awarded a free kick if it was not straight. Now they have given up; the ball is fed in horrendously crooked again."

***Sunday Times* rugby correspondent
Stephen Jones, 21 December 2014.**

"I don't like watching rugby in a hotel where there's public as they come to me and say 'What is that for?' and I don't bloody know. I'm worried about the ruck and maul. I'm worried about players taking players out around the edges of the ruck ... I just get upset with that law where they can knock players over without the ball and it's legal. It's ridiculous. It takes the word sport out of it – it's not sport."

**The late Sir Colin Meads, talking about the "bloody ridiculous" way modern rugby was officiated, May 2015.**

"The sight of superhuman hulks making bone-jarring hits on each other may actually make the game seem more remote than ever. 'Go out and get flattened' is not a selling point to fretting mothers."

**Matt Dickinson, *The Times* chief sports writer, writing on the eve of the 2015 World Cup.**

"The problem is the power is there the whole game. You have 15 players and you can replace half your team. The ball needs to be in play for longer. The more fatigued players are, the more space there is."

**Eddie Jones, talking after masterminding Japan's memorable 34–32 World Cup triumph versus South Africa, October 2015.**

"Rugby union has become a cross between rugby league, with all its long-strung lines of players across the pitch intent on bashing into each other, and American football, with its play book of set pieces which everyone has to learn off by heart. Rugby needs to get back to the times when the tackled player had to release the ball as soon as he was held and his knee hit the floor when, as a result, turnovers were commonplace rather than as rare as hen's teeth."

**Sir Gareth Edwards, February 2016.**

"Do we go back to injury replacements only? Do players need to become more fatigued and not as big and powerful as they are now?"

**A question for the game's lawmakers
from Wales coach Warren Gatland, February 2016.**

"Collision is becoming the legitimate essence of rugby union because the laws are not enforced strictly enough ... Collisions threaten the future of the game."

**Former England fly-half Stuart Barnes
writing in *The Times*, 22 February 2016.**

"When centres and wings are the same weight as amateur-era locks, the evolution of professional rugby has reached a dangerous stage. There are no places of refuge from the onslaught. Anything that encourages downsizing is worth weighing up, so to speak. Rugby must remain about confrontation and courage to go with the myriad skills required but if only the biggest beasts can survive in the jungle, the threat of extinction will grow and grow."

***Daily Mail* rugby correspondent
Chris Foy, 4 March 2016.**

"It is definitely a game of how big can we get players. The main theme is violence at the breakdown for certain directors of rugby. There are coaches who openly talk about the G-force on the hits. I don't know the way forward, I just know that I'm worried, and have been for ages."

**Rugby agent and former Scotland
winger Shaun Longstaff in a BBC Scotland interview,
31 August 2016.**

"Players used to be more aerobic to last the game. Now you can change over half your team, so players play for shorter periods and it's more about power. The hits are relentless from the first to the 80th minute: they used to drop off. By reducing the number of subs, it would change the body type of a player."

**Former England coach Andy Robinson
in *The Times*, 17 September 2016.**

"We do so much in the area of prevention, treatment, management, education around player welfare, we believe the sport has never been safer to play."

**World Rugby CEO Brett Gosper
speaking to CNN *World Sport*, November 2016.**

"For the last four years they have experimented with a return to play protocol for a player who has shown signs and symptoms of concussion and this protocol is not fit for purpose."

**Dr Barry O'Driscoll, who resigned from his role
as World Rugby medical adviser in 2012,
speaking in December 2016.**

"The eight-man bench is currently the main reason why teams can afford muscle-bound forwards who cannot last the pace for the full 80 minutes. It's time to cut the replacements bench back down to size, with a prop who can cover both sides, a hooker, and two more utilities.

"Four replacements would help to restore the aerobic and attritional aspects to rugby union, moving the balance back towards movement rather than muscle. That crucial equilibrium should never have been sacrificed to give coaches excuses to select poorly by giving them half a new team in waiting."

**Rugby correspondent Nick Cain in
*The Rugby Paper*, 5 January 2017.**

"What is the point of a scrum if you have crooked feeds? The laws are clear, but instead we have scrum-halves allowed to put the ball into the second row and hookers who never learn how to hook because they do not have to. The reality is that this is a joke which elite referees have allowed."

**Jeremy Guscott, in his *Rugby Paper* column, 8 January 2017.**

"The not-straight rot has spread to the lineout. It is another variation on turning the set-piece into a win-your-own-ball restart, rather than a contest for possession.

"Elite referees are arguing that they do not want to be responsible for shop-window internationals being ruined by them constantly whistling for set-piece infringements ... My belief is that pro-players are good enough, and are paid enough, to be expected to adapt very quickly ... if it takes a weekend or two of disruption to drum the message home, the time could not have been spent better."

**Nick Cain in *The Rugby Paper*, 17 February 2017.**

"Romain Poite made the headlines with his cracking one-liner, 'I'm a referee. Not a coach' but the plain fact is our referees are doing far too much coaching and not enough refereeing. You see it in virtually every match: a player edges offside at a ruck and the ref warns him to go back."

**Colin Boag, in his column in *The Rugby Paper*, 12 March 2017.**

"Whether it's concussion, or any other injury, the game of rugby is now becoming virtually unplayable ... What we now have is people setting out to collide with each other ... You can't go on playing a game where there is a reasonable expectation that a player who steps out that day is going to get a brain injury."

**Consultant neuropathologist Dr Willie Stewart,
a member of World Rugby's concussion advisory group,
interviewed by BBC Scotland, 21 April 2017.**

"I had guys like Wesley Fofana and Yoann Maestri who played 120 games over three years and turned into grandfathers on the pitch. They had no proper rest, no preparation and were emotionally wrecked."

**Former France coach Philippe Saint-André,
*The Rugby Paper*, 23 April 2017.**

"Something has to give. I'm not saying I'll start it [a players' strike] but I feel like something needs to happen for the suits to realise these guys are serious. It comes down to how much we play. My body could not handle it."

**England and Saracens No 8 Billy Vunipola,
in his book *Wrecking Ball*, September 2017.**

"Every morning I get up, walk down the stairs and I struggle. I'm 34. I had a groin reconstruction, I've got tendonitis in both my Achilles. I've got three prolapsed discs in my spine. We've got a new baby. I can't actually bend over to pick her up. And this is coming from a winger. I wasn't a No 8 who had the huge collisions and competed at the ruck."

**Ugo Monye, speaking on BBC Radio 5 Live's
Weekly Podcast on 12 October 2017.**

"This week, we put out 23 guys against Brive and 17 of them had to report to injury clinic on Sunday and weren't fit to train on Monday morning."

**Worcester lock forward Donncha O'Callaghan, 18 October 2017.**

"Even I'm scared watching the collisions. We've not seen the impact rugby will have on these young men."

**Wales and Lions coach Warren Gatland in a *Guardian* interview, 2 November 2017.**

"When I played, no one tore biceps or hamstrings off the bone. No one had stinger injuries and what is happening is a player's muscular set-up is not natural, while your ligaments and bone structure remain the same. It is the load that causes the problems.

"Twenty-two years on from the arrival of professionalism, I think we are probably paying the price."

**Welsh Rugby Union chairman Gareth Davies, the former Wales fly-half, talking to BBC Wales Live Radio on 9 November 2017.**

"Sort out the thuggery at clear-out time, start reffing it properly. The clear out doesn't exist in law and certainly shouldn't be used as an excuse for players who are not bound to launch themselves off their feet like an Exocet and take out – injure, maim – players who are behind the ball and legally bound on."

**Rugby writer Brendan Gallagher in *The Rugby Paper*, December 2017.**

"We have made excellent player welfare progress, particularly in the priority area of concussion, but we are not complacent; we must ensure that rugby continues to be a leader in sport in the prevention and management of injury."

**Bill Beaumont, after his first full year as World Rugby chairman, 29 December 2017.**

"From 2013 to the current season there's been a 44% increase in contacts. Our average number of contacts per game last season was 600–650 ... but this season we've had over 800 six times and against Exeter we had 1,042 contacts, so you don't have to be a rocket scientist to work out there will be more injuries."

**Bath coach Toby Booth in *The Rugby Paper*, 14 January 2018.**

"This year's Six Nations Championship will be decided through injury. England are without 13 players, Ireland 10, Wales 11, including six first-choice forwards. There is doubt about five of Scotland's front rowers. France are missing 11 key men.

"No club in Britain and Ireland appears unaffected. John Kingston, director of rugby at Harlequins, added up his injured players just before Christmas and counted 23."

***Sunday Times* rugby correspondent Stephen Jones, 28 January 2018.**

"Had someone devised a table for the League of Broken Bones, the Dragons would almost certainly have finished last season top of the pile. According to their medical records, a total of 27 players underwent a total of 32 operations during the course of the campaign ... by the time they had negotiated the first month of last season, the Dragons had a casualty list that stretched to the equivalent of two complete XVs."

**Veteran rugby correspondent Peter Jackson in *The Rugby Paper*, 26 August 2018.**

"Rugby was a game played by 15 players (over a full 80 minutes), who relied on the tactical ability of each player to use his unique skills, maintain his strength, fitness and energy to last for the whole game, while attempting to wear down the opposition, physically and mentally, to take advantage of the final quarter, as the match reached its crescendo.

"Now, we have a squad of 23 allowing over half the team to be replaced by a coach who monitors all for signs of fatigue or failure in his selected group as the game progressed."

**Former England prop forward Jeff Probyn**
**in his column in *The Rugby Paper*, 21 October 2018.**

"Much of the guilt for what has happened, the weaponisation of defences, has come from freedom to play it hard and illegal."

**Former England international Stuart Barnes**
**in *The Times*, 22 October 2018.**

"The one thing I'd really want is that everyone gets 16 weeks break between their last game and their next one. It's a worldwide problem and probably the team that's managing it best at the moment's Ireland. They go 'you can't play' because they own the players and the franchises completely."

**All Blacks coach Steve Hansen**
**calls for a 16-week off season, 28 October 2018.**

"Last week we had the announcement of a new structured season for English rugby hacked out by the Rugby Football Union, Premiership Rugby and the Rugby Players Association (RPA). It was portrayed as some sort of salvation from seasonal savagery. What did we find? Not a single game has been called off, none of the cash cows have been taken to the abattoir and the three bodies have committed despicable atrocity on the Lions, choking them up into an ever smaller and more dangerous area of the season – more of a cat flap than a window."

*Sunday Times* **rugby correspondent Stephen Jones,**
**28 October 2018.**

"While the number of rucks and ball in play time has increased over the past five years, the overall incidence of injury has not increased, which means that the sport's medical standards and injury-prevention programmes in elite adult rugby are having a significantly positive impact."

**World Rugby chief medical officer Dr Martin Raftery**
**addressing the World Rugby Medical Commission**
**Conference in London on 1–2 November 2018.**

*On 9 December 2018, 19-year-old Stade Français back-row forward Nicolas Chauvin was taken unconscious to hospital after his neck was broken in a double tackle playing in a youth match. He died three days later – the third French youngster fatally injured through playing rugby in France in 2018. Widespread calls to make rugby a safer sport followed.*

"Rugby is not a sport where kids should die on the field. There are clear laws that are not always respected. The game was created by an English college as a sport of eluding opponents. It has become a sport of combat. We see game strategies favouring violent collisions rather than the tactics of evasion.

It is important that our rugby becomes a game of movement which limits direct confrontation and charging into each other."

**Retired French neurosurgeon Jean Chazal, sacked by the French Rugby Federation's medical board for his dramatic warning that death was stalking rugby fields, calls for change, December 2018.**

"I am not totally sure I want my son to play rugby."

**French prop Jefferson Poirot, December 2018.**

"Right now, New Zealand rugby is bobbing along above the water, but there is a massive hole in the hull and, just like the *Titanic*, the game here is in danger of sinking. Rugby is categorically not the game of choice for boys aged 13–18. Figures from the last three years show that around 3,000 boys give up rugby between the ages of 10 and 13. Of those still playing at 13, more than half were lost to rugby by the time they were 18. That's not the worst of it, though. The total number of boys playing rugby every year is dropping."

***New Zealand Herald* sports writer Gregor Paul, 1 February 2019.**

"Our view is that the game has actually never been safer than it is now. We were devastated as were the families, the clubs and the union involved... That is a spike that is incredibly unusual... What it does is you make sure that you focus again and keep your focus and your obsession with furthering player welfare."

**World Rugby CEO Brett Gosper, interviewed by RTÉ, Ireland's national broadcaster, after the deaths of four young French rugby players, repeats his 2016 claim rugby union "has never been safer", February 2019.**

"At the breakdown, the letter of the law is you have to bind. Yet no one binds."

**England flanker Sam Underhill highlights an ignored rugby law in *The Rugby Paper*, 10 March 2019.**

"Can we all be wrong?"

**Barry John, speaking to Ross Reyburn in August 2019, questioning why calls to make rugby safer have been ignored by World Rugby.**

"People are dying on rugby pitches. In the seven months between May and December 2018, there were five deaths recorded during a match or as a direct result of playing rugby. Rugby's just a game. It's not worth dying for. And if something isn't done soon, then a professional player will die during a game in front of TV cameras, and only then will people demand that steps must be taken."

**Sam Warburton in his autobiography, *Open Side*, September 2019.**

"One comparison with [World Cup] 1987 which shames the game is there are no more genuine contenders to win the 2019 tournament than there were in 1987. The aspirant countries have had their finances crippled, their best players stolen away. A world game? Possibly, with 90% of the world in chains."

**Sunday Times rugby correspondent Stephen Jones, 15 September 2019.**

"Rugby union is losing its way. There are times when it seems the only purpose of the sport is profit. Professionalism was an anything but smooth journey until recent tragic events [the Covid-19 virus crisis]. The pursuit of profit has poisoned the path it has taken."

**Stuart Barnes in his *Sunday Times* column, 28 June 2020.**

# Contents

1   State of the Union Game   27

2   The Sorry Saga of the Crooked Scrum Feed   32

3   The Concussion Crisis   48

4   Treating Rugby's Battlefield Casualties   57

5   The Great Divide – Union v League   69

6   Farewell Common Sense   89

7   Has Rugby Union Lost its Values?   131

8   The Good and The Bad – The 2019 World Cup   155

9   The End of an Era – 27 August 2020   175

CHAPTER 1

# State of the Union Game

*In March 2016, an open letter signed by 70 academics, doctors and public health professionals argued the game was too dangerous in its existing form to be played in schools.*

"UNLESS THINGS CHANGE, even in the tiny age groups it will only be the big lumps who start to play." Most people dismissed this disturbing view of the future of rugby union expressed by veteran, award-winning *Sunday Times* rugby correspondent Stephen Jones, in June 2015 as unduly alarmist. However exaggerated it seemed, it did reflect the concerns of many leading rugby journalists, ex-players and medical experts, worried how the game's power/skill equation had gone out of kilter, evidenced by the unacceptably high injury count.

A number of positives had thrown a smokescreen over the injury problem, including: the great success of the 2015 World Cup, hosted by England and won by a wonderfully gifted New Zealand side; Ireland's stunning 40–29 win against the All Blacks at Soldier Field, Chicago on 5 November 2016; the excitement generated by Australian Eddie Jones coaching England to 18 successive wins after their dismal exit from the World Cup; an excitingly competitive 2017 Six Nations tournament; and the massive interest in the epic three-Test drawn series between the British & Irish Lions and New Zealand.

However, in 2020 the fact remained, 25 years after the game had turned professional, rugby players were suffering serious injuries at an alarming rate and this was highlighted by the concussion debate and the huge casualty list of leading players unable to play in major tournaments.

As Matt Dickinson, chief sports writer at *The Times*, astutely pointed out, qualifying the huge success of the World Cup in 2015 with more than 2.47 million tickets sold: "The sight of superhuman hulks making bone-jarring hits on each other may actually make the game seem more remote than ever. 'Go out and get flattened' is not a selling point to fretting mothers."

The game's disproportionate emphasis on physicality rather than free-flowing running had been highlighted by the 2017 Six Nations tournament. The gladiatorial Wales v Ireland encounter on 11 March 2017 in Cardiff that brought a 22–9 win for the home side saw a huge total of 341 tackles. Later, on the final day of the tournament, during the France v Wales match in Paris on 18 March, it took a farcical 20 minutes for a controversial scrum duel to be settled at the end of the match.

A year later, during the 2018 Six Nations, Ireland defeated France 15–13 in Paris when fly-half Johnny Sexton landed a superb 45-yard drop kick with the last play of the match. While this kick was a memorable *tour de force*, the prelude offered a revealing insight into the state of modern rugby, for it involved 41 phases with French tacklers downing man after man yet unable to get hold of the ball. For more than five minutes, France had been unable to secure possession and preserve their lead. The match didn't finally end until two minutes and 43 seconds beyond the game's allotted 80 minutes.

Statistics provided a damning indictment of the way the game had been transformed in the professional era, thanks to misguided law changes and toleration of the blatant misuse of existing rules by the International Rugby Board (IRB), renamed World Rugby in 2014. As a result, what had been a highly physical sport in the amateur age became a dangerous sport in the first quarter of a century of the professional era.

In 2019, the collision-based nature of the modern game was

reflected in the fact the tackle count in top level games was quoted as three times higher than in matches in the sport's amateur days. In other words, players in one match were getting through a hugely demanding tackle total that would have taken three games to equal in the amateur days.

This was far from the whole story. Such was the nature of the modern breakdown that players were allowed to continually make illegal clear-out charges, knocking back opponents who hadn't even got the ball without being punished, adding to the physical burden facing the modern player.

In March 2019, former England back Mathew Tait, in his retirement season, offered a stark insight into the demands facing the modern professional rugby player, stating: "The young guys coming through now accept that if they have a ten-year career, of that, probably 20 to 25% of their time is going to be spent injured."

Talk of the upsurge in rugby injuries was nothing new. Three years earlier, in March 2016, Allyson Pollock, professor of public health and research at Queen Mary University of London, had produced an open letter signed by 70 academics, doctors and public health professionals arguing the game was too dangerous in its existing form to be played in schools. It called for a ban on tackling, reverting to touch rugby at school level. After her 14-year-old son Hamish had suffered a broken cheekbone and concussion a year after breaking his leg playing rugby, Pollock had spent a decade researching injuries in school rugby. Her study found pupils had an 11% chance of getting concussed and a 28% chance of getting injured in a school season.

Unhappy as these statistics were, the call for change from a powerful medical lobby did little more than provoke a spirited defence of rugby union and its values. But school rugby was not the only major cause for concern. At the game's top level, the injury statistics had reached an alarmingly high level as during the 2017–18 season, English Aviva Premiership clubs found at least 25% of their playing staff were recovering from injuries suffered in matches or training at any one time.

Neither had the injury crisis ended the frequent repetition of the hollow claim from the game's controlling body, World Rugby: "Player welfare is our No 1 priority." The sheer volume of matches that leading players were expected to play significantly added to the sport's physical demands. From rugby unions and World Rugby came no meaningful attempt to reduce the daunting Test match fixtures treadmill, involving major countries each playing some dozen international matches a year.

On the field, other problems had emerged between 1995 and 2020, involving the application of the laws of the game. The professional era ended the unspoken law of the game's amateur era, that decisions made by the referee should never be disputed. The evidence the game was losing its manners became increasingly evident with players querying refereeing decisions more and more frequently, knowing they could be overturned by the television match official (TMO) consulting video recordings of play.

Bizarrely, rugby union had also become a sport in which you found referees, already burdened with the difficult task of controlling a highly complex sport, not only explaining their decisions but also frequently warning players to abide by the offside laws and other rules during play. "Why?" is the obvious question.

The ultimate example of those controlling the game allowing a crucial law to be ignored was the tolerance among top-level referees of the crooked scrum feed, thus ending one of rugby's most distinctive features.

The unspoken reasoning behind this state of affairs was World Rugby were reluctant to strictly punish every example of law-breaking, as this would create a match of endless stoppages. Besides tolerating offences being a route to anarchy, this contorted logic failed to accept professional players should know the rules of the game they play and abide by them. If the offences were strictly penalised, there would soon be a reduction in stoppages, as was shown when World Rugby eventually decided to strictly penalise the illegal high tackle above shoulder level.

Another major matter of concern was the fact the Pacific Island sides, Fiji, Samoa and Tonga, were still being treated as second-class citizens in financial terms. The result was their hugely talented player base was spread throughout the world with their star players frequently switching allegiance to leading Test nations as well as playing their club rugby abroad.

As the 2018–19 British season got under way, the veteran British rugby writer Stephen Jones produced the ultimate damning indictment of the way the game had been run in the professional era, with commercial imperatives holding sway. He wrote in *The Sunday Times* on 16 September 2018: "The boom at the top end is bogus and robbing the sport of its ethos. And which is worse? Bankruptcy or ushering players to an early grave?"

What follows is a chronicle of the many wrong turns taken in the 25 years since the IRB during a three-day meeting held in Paris in August 1995 finally decided rugby union players could be paid for the first time.

CHAPTER 2

# The Sorry Saga of the Crooked Scrum Feed

*"In every bar, front room and club where games are watched, the crooked feed produces howls of protest."*

THE FIRST MAJOR controversy of rugby union's professional era was provoked by the no doubt well-intentioned but misguided masterplan to give the game greater fluency. Worried that the 15-man game needed to come nearer to matching the quick tempo of its 13-man rival, rugby league, to attract the funding needed to support a professional sport, the International Rugby Board (IRB) allowed the dynamic of the scrum to radically change. The law stating the ball had to be fed straight into the scrum in the middle of the gap between the opposing front rows remained. But the IRB let referees ignore this rule and allow a crooked feed, so scrum-halves could direct the ball towards their own players.

This bizarre example of the IRB failing to uphold one of its own laws brought about the end of a scrum as a hooking contest. The notion this would result in speeding up the game proved a misguided fallacy. What was done had exactly the reverse effect, turning what had been a unique feature of the sport into penalty-seeking shoving contests, with scrum collapses and restarts. The scrum's traditional role of providing backs with quick ball in space unhindered by forwards all but disappeared north of the equator.

What had been a key element of rugby union that made it different to any other sport – two sets of eight forwards locked in combat against each other seeking to gain control of the ball – was now distorted. The crooked feed took away the option of a side not in possession achieving the skilful feat of hooking the ball back, as the ball was placed out of their hooker's reach.

With hooking the ball no longer a contest, the only legal way to secure possession if the other side had the put-in was by out-shoving the opposing pack. With that in mind, front row forwards became bigger and taller and players frequently resorted to illegal tactics to avoid being dominated by a superior pack. The disastrous result of the end of the straight feed was collapsed scrums becoming a common sight, reducing the game's spectator appeal.

Broadcaster and rugby columnist Brian Moore, the formidable England and British & Irish Lions hooker nicknamed Pitbull, who had been a key figure in Will Carling's successful England side that won two Grand Slams and reached the 1991 World Cup final, was a damning critic of the IRB/World Rugby for its failure to uphold its own scrum law. For over a decade, Moore was the main figure campaigning unsuccessfully to end the trashing of the straight put-in law. In 2006, after attending an elite referees' conference, Moore wrote an article headlined "IRB must no longer ignore the scrum issue" that appeared in the *Daily Telegraph* on 18 December stating: "I told the conference this area was becoming a joke and that we will soon end up having rugby league scrums, removing one of the fundamental and unique aspects of rugby union, which is that it is a game for all physiques.

"I said that in every bar, front room and club where games are watched, the crooked feed produces howls of protest. They may not take it seriously, but most other people do.

"Furthermore, their failure to implement this law has had unintended but very serious consequences for the game.

"As the law is not refereed properly it means that a modern

hooker does not have to be a hooker at all in the traditional sense. He no longer has to strike the ball, needing only to move his foot a few inches, knowing the ball will appear behind his foot in any event. This has led to many teams playing big men who often look like Dan Quayle under interrogation when they get the ball in loose play.

"In addition, because the feeds are so bad it is no longer possible to strike for the ball on the opposition put-in. This has led to one-dimensional power scrummaging where the only imperative is to hit as hard as you can and keep the weight on throughout the scrum. From an early age this is all that is done when it comes to scrummaging.

"So what? Well, this is what – there are an increasing number of younger props who are retiring early because of back problems caused by this unsophisticated scrummaging."

Moore, a qualified solicitor, with withering logic highlighted the fact a law was being ignored.

"I also questioned what right referees, even elite ones, have to simply ignore and by omission refuse to properly implement any law of rugby. Either it is a law, or it is not. If the former, it should be applied, if the latter, it should be removed completely, but to have a law honoured only in the breach is ridiculous."

The conference also heard Steve Walsh, the New Zealand referee, highlighting the totally unreasonable dilemma facing match officials, saying he was prepared to referee the put-in properly but was not going to award ten free kicks and find himself dropped from the panel of elite referees.

The conference appeared to back Moore's stance with Dr Syd Millar, then chairman of the IRB, giving an assurance the law would be applied come January 2007. But Moore, correctly, was unconvinced forecasting: "I fear that it was all talk, and that nothing will happen."

And so it proved. Six years later, on 28 March 2013, Moore could be found investigating what had gone wrong with this feature of the union game in a Radio 5 Live programme titled

*The Scrum.* In an article on the **BBC** Sports website publicising the broadcast, he produced yet another damning indictment on the subject stating: "Instead of being a means of restarting the game, it has become a way of winning penalties. To be frank, the whole edifice has become a grotesque farce and is blighting the game. Not only has the scrum become tedious, but it is dangerous. Ironically, the solution is the simple application of the existing laws."

Hosting the programme, the charmingly polite Eleanor Oldroyd, who seemed somewhat over anxious to portray guests at obvious loggerheads with each other as "singing from the same hymn sheet", failed to decipher the mystery of why the straight scrum feed had become the law that dares not speak its name. Two great servants of rugby, Welshman Nigel Owens, regarded as the world's best rugby referee, and IRB representative John Jeffrey, the great Scotland blindside flanker christened the Great White Shark in a Test career that ended in 1991, were questioned by former England and Lions front row forwards Moore and Phil Vickery. And both, deserting their commanding on-the-field personas, were sheepishly apologetic and at a loss in effectively justifying the IRB's failure to enforce its own scrum feed law.

The much-admired authority and wit displayed by Owens ("If you are going to cheat, cheat fairly") on a rugby field was absent when Moore asked who from the IRB had given a blanket instruction telling elite referees to ignore the straight put-in law.

"Who tells us to ignore the crooked feed?" Owens queried, sounding totally surprised as if he had been struck by a verbal thunderbolt.

"Yeah," said Moore.

"Nobody," replied Owens. "I certainly haven't been told that. I am not making excuses. It is an area of the game we need to improve on and referee better. Sometimes I go home and look at a game and say 'How the hell did I miss that crooked feed?' I am looking at so many things going on in the scrum it is down the checklist of priorities. That's not an excuse. It's in the laws and we need to referee it and we need to be better at it."

Jeffrey, as a member of the IRB's Scrum Steering Group which was examining ways of making the scrum safer and more effective, was equally apologetic.

"I couldn't agree with you more," Jeffrey told the two formidable former England front row forwards and emphasised his wish to see the straight feed restored. "The scrum is a blight on our game – it has to be sorted."

Asked how the crooked feed had been allowed to become the norm, he replied somewhat bewilderingly: "It is just the way the game has evolved."

But he did offer a disturbing clue as to why the state of affairs had continued saying: "I've spoken to most of the Tier One coaches in the last month and, believe it or not, none of them want a straight put-in. The coaches say they want to guarantee the feed, which is bizarre."

One was left wondering whether coaches rather than the IRB were dictating the laws of rugby union. Did Jeffrey not realise coaches opposed the straight feed being enforced as it would mean changing their coaching techniques through the return of competitive hooking? Further quizzed by Vickery on why the IRB didn't just tell referees to enforce the existing straight feed law, Jeffrey somewhat mystifyingly said nothing could be done until the results of a global trial seeking to make the scrum safer were available and the whole scrum legislation could be assessed. Quite why this reasoning justified an existing law being totally ignored was another matter.

Three years later, in March 2016, with the crooked feed virtually never penalised, Moore was again quizzing Owens as he entered the dock on another Radio 5 Live Sport programme as to why the straight feed law was being ignored. Again, the popular Welshman was in a defensive, apologetic mode saying:

"Brian, I agree with you 100% ... we need to get better", adding: "Believe me it is not a simple as it looks."

Rugby union is a very complex game and it is difficult to think of any other sport that demands so much of match officials. But judging sending the ball down the middle of the scrum tunnel posed no great problem during the long history of the sport, until the 21st century. Admittedly, after the game turned professional, refereeing scrums became that much more difficult. Players were more powerful and bigger than their amateur predecessors, with weightlifting viewed a vital part of training as out-shoving opponents became the key to keeping or gaining possession, while the art of hooking did a gradual disappearing act. Packs no longer staged scrums in double-quick time, completing the process unaided by referees, and illegalities became ever more frequent.

Scrums were a complex process and the Nigel Owens view that his priorities lay with ensuring scrums were conducted safely without collapsing needs to be respected. However, if the referees found it hard to police the feed effectively, there was a straightforward solution freeing them from this responsibility. A striking feature of the modern rugby era was the outstanding television coverage of major matches, with cameras trained on seemingly every aspect of the game all too clearly highlighting crooked scrum feeds. Why not simply end the controversy by getting the TMO to tell the referee "Crooked feed" on his microphone when the law was broken?

In 2013, Stephen Jones, the award-winning *Sunday Times* rugby correspondent, was equally scathing while reporting on a Harlequins v Bath encounter: "I calculated from 18 scrums the ball emerged for play to continue four times. It was a crabbing, cheating mess, beyond frustration. The scrum has been a disaster for years, chiefly because the International Rugby Board (IRB) has disgracefully allowed referees to ignore the law."

The ultimate example of the destruction of the traditional scrum came in the France v Wales match on the final day of the Six Nations tournament on 18 March 2017 when it took a farcical eight resets and 20 minutes to resolve the scrum duel that ended the game, with not one straight scrum feed to offer the defending side a chance to hook the ball. The post-match accusations that France had cheated by returning a powerful prop to the field as a substitute, and that winger George North had been bitten by a Frenchman, obscured the far more significant fact that the modern scrum had become a blight on the sport.

If the laws of the game had been applied properly, the match would have ended after one scrum, with Wales being awarded a free kick for a crooked feed by the French scrum-half and just kicking the ball into touch to win the game. But there was no way referee Wayne Barnes could have taken this option, as World Rugby had spent years getting elite referees to ignore the straight feed law. Amid the chaos, Barnes stayed commendably cool. But forgetting the straight feed law as he had to, he could have ended the game by awarding France a penalty try rather than a succession of penalties that resulted in scrum resets. He judged that the Welsh forwards were continually illegally disrupting the scrum as they were being driven back towards the try line. How many times should teams be allowed to illegally halt try-scoring opportunities before incurring a penalty try?

Ironically, back in 2013 as the leading English referee, Barnes had loftily announced there would be zero tolerance of crooked feeds.

That year, the IRB significantly countered the spate of collapsed scrums by introducing the "Crouch, bind, set" instruction. This welcome initiative didn't end scrum problems but it did significantly stabilise this feature of the game. The fact some referees seemed to take an age issuing the instruction with a long pause between each command was understandable as safety was the overriding concern in a complex feature of the game where power counted.

Allied to the new scrum formation commands, the IRB also attempted to end the crooked put-ins blighting the game. This welcome decision was made clear by Barnes when he told the media: "We've been asked as a priority from the International Rugby Board to get the ball in straight. We know the media and the fans have been crying out for that. Our priority is the scrum feed. We don't want to start off by being very hard in week one then by week 20 everyone's forgotten about it."

But the return of the straight feed by simply upholding the existing law proved all too brief. South African Craig Joubert provided a startling example of how short-lived the initiative proved. In what was the first international under the new laws, with Australia playing New Zealand, he penalised four crooked scrum feeds in the first 11 scrums. In the next 12 matches, he handled 143 scrums without penalising a single scrum feed.

Why the IRB directive was ignored so quickly remained a mystery. No doubt the view of All Blacks scrum guru Mike Cron, a member of the Scrum Steering Group, as the main man wanting to eliminate the straight put-in on safety grounds, proved influential. The fact coaches were in favour of crooked scrum feeds assuring possession for their side was another key factor in the law continuing to be ignored, for World Rugby in their role as gatekeeper of the game's laws seemed obsessed with ruling by consensus, avoiding decisions that would attract opposition.

The sheer hypocrisy of this situation was pointed out to me by a former senior English referee I used to play club cricket with, before his career took him to a post as an IT systems manager in Paris in 1989, where he has remained ever since. An Oxford graduate who had kept wicket for the university against the 1964 Australian tourists, Andrew Mason was an outstanding club cricketer, voted Midland Clubman of the Year in 1971 after Moseley Ashfield won the inaugural Midland Club

Championship under his captaincy. Four years later he scored 1,508 runs in a season, averaging 47, a feat that still remains a record for the club where England all-rounder Moeen Ali was a youth cricketer three decades later. Mason was also a talented rugby player. But his first XV appearances for Moseley were limited as the West Midlands club's main full-back was the late Sam Doble, one of the game's great kickers who landed 14 points in his Test debut in 1972 when England surprised the rugby world beating South Africa 18–9 in Johannesburg.

Injuries led to Mason taking up refereeing and he spent many years officiating at the top of English rugby, including handling the 1991 Middlesex Sevens final won by London Scottish defeating Harlequins 20–16 and being a touch judge when France were beaten for the first time on home soil by Romania in 1990. In 1999, he became a referee supervisor for the French Rugby Federation, a post he still holds.

In the summer of 2017, he told me his overall assessment of the referee's performance was not influenced by how the ball was fed into the scrum. "Most reports I write contain the statement 'The referee did not concern himself with the put-in', although the more grotesque introductions do get penalised and I can then remain silent. When I started, I would discuss the fact [that the ball is not put in straight] face-to-face but I soon became aware that it was considered normal and that I was not supposed to allow it to affect my judgment of the referee's overall performance."

Despite the blatant failure to enforce its own scrum feed law, World Rugby offered the public neither explanation nor justification for the chaos it caused. What did World Rugby expect coaches to tell schoolboy scrum-halves learning the game? Feed the ball in straight as the law requires or just follow the example set by leading players and put the ball in crooked? It was difficult to avoid the damning conclusion that too often World Rugby felt no need to justify the way it was running the game as it had been content to simply ignore adverse comments about its rulings from some of the sport's most respected figures.

The experiences of Colin Boag, a rugby correspondent with *The Rugby Paper*, offered a vivid insight into the futility of trying to penetrate World Rugby's wall of silence surrounding exactly why one of the laws that made rugby such a distinctive sport was not enforced. In April 2016, he wrote in his column: "One of the areas that baffles and infuriates most rugby supporters is the apparent contradiction between Law 20.6 which says: 'The scrum-half must throw in the ball straight down the middle line immediately beyond the width of the nearest prop's shoulders' and what they see with their own eyes week after week.

"The scrum feed has become a standing joke within the game. Last year there was a subtle change inasmuch as the scrum feed no longer needs to be straight but 'credible' whatever that means.

"Back in February I set out to try properly to understand the advice given to referees on the scrum feed and it has been a total nightmare. First the Rugby Football Union asked that I wait until the Six Nations was over – I am not sure why but maybe they don't do multi-tasking – and despite my bafflement I went along with it. When I went back after the tournament, they changed tack and said I needed to approach World Rugby, so I did and got nowhere.

"I sent about a dozen emails, and made numerous phone calls, and got bounced back to the RFU. I had assumed, wrongly as it turned out, the authorities would welcome the opportunity to shed some light on the problem but clearly not."

After again returning to the RFU, Boag did get a reply of sorts from Tony Spreadbury, the RFU's man in charge of elite referees, who assured him, "The putting the ball into the scrum is an important area of the game. We want to encourage a contest and that there is a credible feed. Some teams have decided that the hooker hooks for the ball and others want to drive over the ball."

But what was meant by "a credible feed" remained unexplained leaving the obvious conclusion it was a crooked feed in disguise.

Eventually Boag did find "someone who knows but wouldn't speak on the record" confirming "if any part of the ball travels down the middle line [of a scrum], that's good enough. So, when we see the ball being fed into the tunnel, it can be almost a foot from the centre and still be legal by the way Law 20.6 is now being interpreted."

To get a free kick, Boag was told, the feed had to be "so crooked it's laughable".

Boag was not alone in failing to get answers to fundamental questions about the way the game is controlled by World Rugby. As a freelance journalist back in 2015, I sent several emails to Dominic Rumbles, World Rugby's head of communications, asking what I mistakenly believed were four straightforward questions about rugby laws not being enforced. Mysteriously, Rumbles, after querying my journalistic credentials, was able to reply to my two emails asking if he had received my questions, but stated he had not received my original email containing the questions. The fact I returned his second email adding the questions was not enough to get a reply. I then sent a registered letter with the questions to Rumbles at his Dublin office, that was duly signed for, and also left a message on his answer phone. I finally surrendered after neither brought a reply. The message was all too clear: don't be surprised if you are ignored if you ask World Rugby awkward questions.

To its credit, World Rugby with its "Crouch, bind, set" instruction ended forwards crashing into each other to set up scrums and scrums wheeling out of kilter even before the feed, as happened in the game's amateur era. But the crooked feed continued to be ignored in the game's top flight.

In August 2017, World Rugby introduced a law amendment enabling scrum-halves to make a straight feed nearer their own front row rather than down the middle of the tunnel between the two opposing sets of forwards. It ruled the scrum-half must put the ball in straight but allowed him to align a shoulder with the middle of the scrum rather than placing his whole body facing the centre line. Effectively this meant the scrum-half was putting the ball into his own side of the scrum, making his own hooker's task that much easier. Thus, the ball was landing the length of the scrum-half's shoulder – inches rather than feet – away from the centre line of the tunnel, partially, at least, in what had traditionally been crooked feed territory.

The reasoning behind this scrum feed change, according to World Rugby, was "to promote scrum stability, a fair contest for possession while also giving the advantage to the team throwing in." How feeding it so near your own front row could be termed "a fair contest for possession" took some figuring out.

Anyone with a basic knowledge of how the traditional scrum worked could tell you a quality hooker in the amateur era didn't need that amount of help to win the ball and would view this law change as promoting an unfair rather than fair contest. With a traditional, straight scrum feed, the team awarded the scrum still had a considerable advantage, as shown by the fact that strikes against the head were regarded as a significant achievement by the hooking fraternity.

In the clubhouse after a match in the distant past, it was not hard to find front row forwards in a world of their own talking about the results of the scrum contest. Say a 3–1 win was being discussed, this was not some football result but the fact your front row had won a vital three strikes against the head to one by their opponents in the scrum battle.

The intention of the law change may have been seemingly in the best interests of the game, as at least in theory it retained a straight scrum feed and made the game safer. Unfortunately, the reality was rather different in terms of the straight feed. Rather than promoting a "fair" contest for the ball, World

Rugby found the new scrum law backfired, signalling the death of the art of hooking.

The plan may have been to revive the straight scrum feed by allowing the scrum-half to feed the ball nearer his own front row, but this was just ignored by players and not enforced by referees. Scrum-halves, able to get nearer their front row, just blatantly abused the new law and fed the ball straight into their scrum so it could be heeled back without being contested by the opposition.

When I spoke to Andrew Mason again in 2020, he narrated how in assessing the performance of referees in France he found there was no longer any point in the opposition trying to hook the ball as the law amendment was being ignored. In his words: "The idea of the change was to stop the crooked feed. What scrum-halves are supposed to do is be square-on, closer to their own front row and send the ball in straight into the tunnel parallel to the goal line. But they don't. They stand half a metre to the right, which the new law allows, but rarely send in the ball parallel to the goal line as the law requires. The opposition have no chance of hooking the ball and don't really try.

"Very few referees I have come across at any level are respecting the straight feed law. I don't believe anybody has actually said ignore the law either verbally or in writing. It is just a fact. Almost nobody is enforcing the straight feed law with any degree of determination. The only time a referee penalises a crooked feed is when the feed is so grotesque it is difficult to ignore."

On 19 April 2020 in *The Rugby Paper*, the much admired British rugby columnist Nick Cain and scrum guru Phil Keith-Roach, scrum coach for England's 2003 World Cup winning team, offered a shrewd analysis of the problems facing this distinctive feature of the union code in a feature headlined "So how do you fix this mess called the scrum?" Cain pointed out that the paper's postbag, as well as rugby social media comment forums, were overflowing with complaints from supporters deeply disillusioned with the degrading of the scrum "especially the recent law change that allows crooked or 'favourable' put-ins when the scrum-half is able to sidestep towards his own hooker."

The duo listed a major problem as the "incredibly convoluted series of up to seven stages" before the put-in, starting with players ambling towards the mark called by the referee with no sense of urgency. By contrast in the amateur era scrums formed up rapidly needing no directions from the referee. Calling for players to be responsible for forming up quickly for a scrum, Keith-Roach argued: "All you need is a controlled engagement. That's it. If you looked at the games between England and New Zealand from 1997 to 2000 the scrums were over within 30 seconds."

The transformation of the scrum into a shambles in the professional era had people even lobbying for this distinctive feature of the union game to be abandoned altogether and replaced with league's tap-and-go restart. However, this would provide a fundamental unwanted change to the nature of rugby union, for no longer would backs have the wide spaces to operate in created by having 16 forwards interlocked in a scrum in a small area of the pitch.

Part of rugby union's appeal is the fact that it has always been termed "a sport for all sizes". Before power became the major priority in the scrum, it was easy to recognise front row forwards as they were generally smaller in height and much bulkier than their second row and back row colleagues in the pack. And they were regarded as great characters, operating on rugby's coalface in a tough world of their own.

My father, New Zealand-born writer Wallace Reyburn, who covered the Seventh All Blacks tour of Britain in 1972–73 for his book *The Winter Men*, offered an interesting insight into the fact some front row rugby forwards could be a little down to earth compared with their team colleagues.

45

In the earlier stage of the tour, my father made the mistake of trying to talk to the formidable New Zealand prop forward Keith Murdoch, later christened rugby's Wild Man and sent home in disgrace for assaulting people off the field.

When my father approached Murdoch simply stating his name and the fact he was doing a book on the tour, he was told: "F*** off!"

In his wonderfully evocative book *Stand Up and Fight – When Munster Beat the All Blacks*, Irish sportswriter Alan English also recalled the incident in print, adding: "Wallace Reyburn did as he was bid."

My father remained philosophical about the incident, writing: "One thing could be said for this exchange. At least we knew where we stood. From then on we were in amicable agreement. He went his way and I went mine."

What went on in a scrum was often regarded as a mystery to the average back, but they were not the only ones in the dark. Andrew Mason recalled in the distant past being with fellow referees seeking to gain a helpful insight into the dark arts of front row play by talking to a player with an impressive playing CV. Cambridge Blue Nick Drake-Lee, at the age of 20, was the youngest prop forward to play for England when he made his Test debut in his country's 13–6 victory against Wales at Cardiff Arms Park on 19 January 1963. That year, England went on to win the Five Nations Championship and the young Leicester forward was to win a further seven caps.

Talking to Mason and his fellow referees, Drake-Lee delivered the not entirely reassuring verdict: "You shouldn't be surprised if you don't know why the scrum's gone down because we hardly ever know why!"

Twenty-five years into rugby's professional era, the scrum controversy had acquired backwater status, ceasing to be a major talking point as the long, unsuccessful battle to restore the art of hooking had lost impetus. Scrum collapses were no longer a disturbing feature of matches thanks to successful law changes and leading rugby broadcasters and commentators had mostly given up complaining about crooked feeds.

Rugby's major concern had switched to the unacceptable injury levels in the sport, highlighted by alarming concussion statistics. And those who had lamented the fact the scrum had radically changed in the professional era at least had the consolation of knowing it was still an important feature of rugby union, as shown by the fact South Africa's dominant scrum proved the key factor in their 32–12 victory over England in the 2019 World Cup final in Japan.

CHAPTER 3

# The Concussion Crisis

*"We can't have a game where the end product is a brain-damaged super-human who's made a bit of money"*

RUGBY UNION'S HUGE rise in popularity in the professional era was sadly matched by a rising injury toll, with the major concern being that too many players were getting concussed. While problems with the scrum were the main focus in the first decade of the 21st century, the realisation came in the second decade that, with the ever-increasing emphasis on power, rugby had become a dangerous game.

A World Rugby database of 1,526 professional matches played between 2013 and 2015 showed there had been 611 head injury assessments. Commendable though World Rugby's efforts may have been to ensure that head injury assessments (HIAs) meant players didn't remain on the field or return to play after being concussed, the effectiveness of the assessment was too often debatable.

The tests originated in August 2012 as Pitch-Side Concussion Assessments (PSCAs), requiring players to remain off the field for a minimum of five minutes after a suspected concussion collision. They soon attracted high profile adverse publicity when Dr Barry O'Driscoll resigned as the medical adviser for the International Rugby Board (before it became World Rugby) and produced a withering indictment of the new measure.

Criticising the IRB thinking as fundamentally flawed,

he said: "If a player needs to undergo a PSCA, he must, by definition, be showing signs of concussion. And as soon as he is showing symptoms, he should not be allowed to play on. For many years now, research into concussion has made it clear that anybody suspected of concussion, showing any signs or symptoms, should come off the field and should not go back."

It was hardly difficult to find examples of high-profile players confirming O'Driscoll's reasoning by being returned to the game after appearing to be concussed, despite the assessment procedures. On 6 July 2013, early on in the third Test in Sydney when the British & Irish Lions defeated Australia 41–16, the outstanding Australian flanker George Smith was involved in an awful clash of heads with the Lions hooker Richard Hibbard. Television viewers could clearly see Smith seemed to be concussed as, even ignoring his dazed state, he was obviously unsteady on his feet as he was helped off the field. But having passed the PSCA test, he later was allowed to rejoin the game.

Smith's own recollection highlighted how ridiculous it was allowing his return to the game: "You saw me snake dancing off the field. I passed the [concussion] tests that were required within those five minutes and I got out there."

After the Smith incident, Dr O'Driscoll sent an email to the Australian Brett Gosper, the IRB's chief executive officer, repeating his call for a new approach. He wrote: "My views on suspected concussion in rugby are well known and documented within the IRB. They were the reason for my resignation. The five-minute assessment of a player who has demonstrated distinct signs of concussion for 60 to 90 seconds and usually longer, is totally discredited. There is no scientific, medical or rugby basis for the safety of this process. This experiment, which is employed by no other sport in the world, is returning the player to what is an extremely brutal arena."

In August 2014, the PSCA officially changed into the more detailed Head Injury Assessment (HIA) involving ten rather than five minutes off the pitch for cognitive, balance and memory tests. As well as showing no obvious signs of concussion, such as blurred vision, drowsiness or nausea, the player had to answer simple questions such as "What venue are you at?" and "Which half is it?" The tests also included remembering a sequence of five words and then repeating them in reverse. And there was a balance test involving walking forwards, placing one foot directly in front of the other.

But this more detailed examination didn't prevent the Northampton, Wales and Lions wing George North being returned to play on two occasions after being involved in alarming head collisions. One of the world's most devastating attackers, North, a giant of a man standing at 1.94m (6ft 4in) and weighing 120kg (19st), who scored 36 tries for his country in 80 appearances from 2010 to 2018, was floored by blows to his head five times in less than two seasons. On 6 February 2015 while playing for Wales he suffered an accidental kick to the head during the first half of a 21–16 loss to England at the Millennium Stadium. After an assessment he returned to the field and he continued playing again after receiving a second blow to the head in the same game.

On 3 December 2016, playing for Northampton against Leicester at Welford Road, he again was returned to the field after an HIA. He had been taken off after lying, eyes closed on the ground as a result of landing on his head after a mid-air collision with the Leicester wing Adam Thompstone, while trying to catch the ball. On North's return in that Northampton match, Dr O'Driscoll told the CNN *World Sport* show: "World Rugby are totally to blame for this. For the last four years they have experimented with a return to play protocol for a player who has shown signs and symptoms of concussion and this protocol is not fit for purpose."

After a two-week investigation into the incident, the concussion management review group, a panel formed by the Rugby Football Union and Premiership Rugby, found

Northampton wrongly allowed North to return to the pitch at Leicester after he had appeared to lose consciousness. But in an act of disturbing judicial largesse that did little for the image of the sport, it was decided Northampton should not be penalised, as the review group did not consider that the club's medical team failed to complete the HIA protocol nor intentionally ignored the player's best interests.

The Rugby Players Association (RPA) in a tactful condemnation of the fence-sitting verdict of the review group said sanctions, had they been applied, would have sent a "clear message" about the "gravity of concussion management".

Former Scotland international John Beattie, a leading campaigner for the welfare of rugby players, who provided a disturbing insight into the consequences of concussion in his *Panorama* special *Rugby and the Brain – Tackling the Truth*, which screened on BBC1 in September 2015, was equally concerned.

"We can't have a game where the end product is a brain-damaged super-human who's made a bit of money," the 59-year-old told BBC Radio 5 Live. "I know blokes my age and younger who have brain damage. I worry about George North. I think we need to be much more careful with players."

As for the idea that North had supposedly told the medics he had not lost consciousness, Beattie's view was "the last person you should listen to is the player" as they are "trapped in a money-earning spiral".

Dr O'Driscoll shared the same view: "We have all seen players who have appeared fine five minutes after a concussive injury then vomited later in the night." He also agreed with Beattie that players' accounts should not be accepted as they were not always acting in their own best interests. His second cousin, the great Irish international Brian O'Driscoll, provided the evidence of this in his autobiography *The Test* (2015) outlining how he was able to return to the field to play for Ireland after convincing medics he was fit to resume, when he should be have remained sidelined.

"It's only afterwards that I'm in a position to see things with clarity and accept that the decision – always – has got to be taken out of our [the players'] hands," O'Driscoll wrote.

A month before the Northampton episode involving North, World Rugby's CEO Brett Gosper, a former Australian rugby trialist who enjoyed a hugely successful career in marketing, told the media: "Player welfare is our No 1 priority. We do so much in the area of prevention, treatment, management, education around player welfare, we believe the sport has never been safer to play."

Whatever the medical shortcomings of the HIAs, World Rugby did deserve credit for at least getting more players with suspected concussion off the field for an assessment. When Dr O'Driscoll worked with the IRB in 2012, 56% of players who passed an assessment on the field of play were later determined to have suffered concussion. But with HIAs, the number of players mistakenly returned to play had dropped to 4%. This lower figure could hardly be described as acceptable, but it at least showed a dramatic change for the better.

However, the numbers of players suffering head injuries was growing alarmingly, so taking concussed players out of the firing line could hardly be equated with preventing players getting injured in the first place. Gosper's claim that rugby was "safer than ever" was plainly absurd, not least because research backed by his own organisation contradicted his claim. In November 2017, Dr Izzy Moore, a sport and exercise medicine lecturer from Cardiff Metropolitan University, revealed reported concussions had increased by 172% in four seasons. This worrying statistic came from research funded not only by the Welsh Rugby Union but also World Rugby itself.

Neither did Gosper's assertion "We do so much in the area of prevention" seem to have applied in the case of the courageous Wales and Lions full-back Leigh Halfpenny. You would not think that leading professional rugby players would have a basic flaw in their tackle technique. But this was the case with Halfpenny, who was prone to making the cardinal error of placing his head in front rather than by the side of or behind the player he was tackling. The unfortunate end result was the player he tackled colliding with his head and the severity of the impact more than once left him concussed. The fact a player as gifted as Halfpenny was seen by millions making a schoolboy error was disturbing to say the least. Why had coaches not remedied this obvious technical flaw on the training ground?

A study of Premiership Rugby in England concluded that rates of concussion had gone from 6.7 concussions per 1,000 player hours in 2012–13 to 15.8 concussions per 1,000 player hours in 2015. Concussion accounted for 25% of the total of all match-day injuries.

The drama of the 2017 Six Nations tournament obscured the worrying statistic that Scotland had no less than a total of seven players taken off the field due to concussion in just two matches against France and England.

Dr O'Driscoll was not the only medical expert highly critical of the efforts of World Rugby to reduce concussion problems. Interviewed by BBC Scotland in April 2017, Dr Willie Stewart, a member of World Rugby's independent concussion advisory group, said attempts to tackle the issues around brain injuries had had little effect. He also described HIAs as "not fit for purpose".

"Whether it's concussion, or any other injury, the game of rugby is now becoming virtually unplayable," said Dr Stewart, a consultant neuropathologist and former amateur rugby player.

The fact so many of the game's leading players, such New Zealand's legendary flanker Richie McCaw and No 8 Kieran Read, Welsh trio North, Halfpenny and flanker Sam Warburton and Ireland backs Brian O'Driscoll and Johnny

Sexton, had all been sidelined from playing due to concussion threw a spotlight on the crisis. And the number of concussions occurring did not reveal the true extent of the problem as the figures did not show the damage done by players relentlessly colliding with each other. You don't have to be knocked out to damage your brain.

In October 2016 in his column in *The Rugby Paper*, the former Wales winger Shane Williams, scorer of 58 tries in 87 internationals, revealed his own highly disturbing playing experiences, saying: "Goodness knows how many bangs I took to the head. But the truth is that I probably suffered a concussion-type injury once every three games I played. That's no exaggeration and over a 15-year career that's a lot of bangs to the head."

As one of the game's great wingers, Williams was not directly involved in rugby's main physical battlefront involving the forwards, so his revelations offered an alarming insight into the game's physicality. Wales and Lions captain Sam Warburton, who was stretchered off the field suffering from concussion during his country's 25–21 2016 Six Nations defeat at Twickenham, also tellingly highlighted how forwards endure head bangs in top flight rugby to a worrying degree.

"The breakdown is a pretty ugly place when you've got three 18-stoners flying in, trying to take your head off," he said, when interviewed in 2014. "Sometimes I'm struggling to shampoo my head the next day because my head is hurting so bad."

Rugby's transition, since turning professional in 1995, into a sport of extreme physical contact demanding an unprecedented level of physical courage, was highlighted by the significantly increased size of leading players and the fact that a tackle was frequently referred to as a "hit".

But the trend was far from irreversible. January 2017 offered a seemingly minor but telling indication how it could be relatively easy to make the game of rugby safer. As 2016 neared a close, World Rugby announced that from 3 January 2017 there would be a "zero-tolerance approach" to players making reckless tackles that hit the neck or head area, instructing referees to issue yellow or red cards. They also ruled legitimate tackles accidently sliding up to the head and neck could be punished with a penalty. There was heavy criticism of the directive being issued in mid-season, forcing players to adopt a "new" approach to tackling. Initially matches produced a spate of yellow plus several red cards, alongside accusations the game was "going soft".

On 13 January 2017, the sight of South African international François Steyn being sent off by JP Doyle, after felling Johnny Sexton with a flaying arm to the neck after the Ireland fly-half had passed the ball in the Montpellier v Leinster Champions Cup game in France, sent a clear signal players would no longer get away with careless dangerous tackles. And the message became even clearer when Steyn was handed a four-week ban for the tackle.

A few weeks after World Rugby's directive came into force, the fuss died down and suddenly rugby felt just a little safer as players stuck to the existing tackle law and avoided the risk of being banished from the field for 10 minutes with a yellow card for a high tackle, or for the whole game with a red card. *Daily Telegraph* columnist Brian Moore, England's outstanding hooker in the Will Carling era, neatly answered critics of the new directive writing: "What happened is that officials were given a reminder of their duty to apply the sanctions for high tackles – there was no new law as such ... Nor is it useful to allege rugby has gone soft. It is sufficiently hard, and will remain so, without headshot tackles. There is nothing tough or brave about them."

In fact, before the new directive came into force, referees were taking a noticeably stronger line on reckless play. In December 2016, the formidable Leicester and England centre Manu Tuilagi, making yet another sadly unsuccessful comeback from injury, was yellow carded twice in successive weeks for shoulder-charging opponents who didn't have the ball.

"I think we'll be playing touch rugby soon. The rules have changed … it's soft now – soft cards," was Tuilagi's verdict on the two decisions. Did he really feel flooring an opponent, who had passed the ball, with a rampaging shoulder charge, as happened with his second yellow card, was acceptable? Ignoring the fact it was illegal in rugby union terms, would he advocate schoolkids following his example?

The most significant example of the effectiveness of the new high tackle directive came on 1 July 2017 when New Zealand centre Sonny Bill Williams was given a red card for a reckless shoulder charge tackle which crashed into the head of winger Anthony Watson after 24 minutes of the British & Irish Lions' second Test against the All Blacks. The Lions went on to win the match 24–21 at Wellington, and so levelled the series.

No one would argue this directive had a major impact by reducing rugby's injury problems. It did nothing to halt the sheer volume and physicality of the tackle count found in modern games. However, the directive did provide an interesting indication that players were far more likely to abide by the game's laws if they were enforced. But, as was shown in the 2019 World Cup, it took almost another three years before a true zero-tolerance approach was adopted in an effort to enforce an existing law and thereby make the game less hazardous.

CHAPTER 4

# Treating Rugby's
# Battlefield Casualties

*"The human body is not meant to take that amount of force."*

DESPITE SPORT BEING a major cause of injuries, sports medicine
was a relatively new speciality that had played an ever more
important role in seeking to make rugby union a safer game.
There was plenty of evidence that measures needed to be taken.
In a review spanning the 2007–2017 decade, the Institute of
Sport and Exercise Medicine at South Africa's Stellenbosch
University concluded: "Over the years, rule changes were
introduced to minimize the risk of serious injury and to keep
the ball in play. Despite these efforts, compared with other
collision sports, including American football, injury rates in
rugby union remain roughly three times higher."

It had not always been so. In British rugby's amateur era,
injuries were rarely on the media radar and few viewed injury
levels as a major concern. No medical specialists were assigned
to matches and injured players in major matches were revived
with the "magic sponge" – a sponge dipped into a bucket of
cold water, usually brought onto the field by a middle-aged
clubman with no medical qualifications.

On a sunny Monday morning in February 2019, I drove to
the district of Cefn Mably set in picturesque rolling countryside
six miles north of the Welsh capital Cardiff, to visit the home of
the man who has played a pioneering role in developing sports
medicine in the UK.

In 2011, consultant orthopaedic surgeon Professor John Fairclough was hailed by *The Times* newspaper as one of the UK's top 50 surgeons through his achievements spanning 30 years of working with the sports medicine team at Cardiff Metropolitan University. It was in the university's biomechanical lab that he developed advanced knee surgery techniques with his colleague Professor Charles Archer, and the elite athletes he treated included England rugby's Jonny Wilkinson and Welshmen, Olympic hurdler Colin Jackson and former world champion boxer Joe Calzaghe.

A former president of the British Sports Trauma Association, Professor Fairclough served on the Welsh RFU medical committee for 20 years and was awarded an honorary fellowship by the Cardiff Metropolitan University for his medical achievements.

It was in the early 1980s that Professor Fairclough and his friend Dr Roger Evans, head of a Cardiff hospital's accident and emergency department, broke new ground by attending Cardiff Rugby Club's matches and providing expert medical treatment for injured players.

"In those days, Roger and I were both rugby players who were interested in following Cardiff," he recalled when we met. "We felt there was a need to have a medical presence at the matches. They were just very pleased to have someone who was happy do deal with them on a regular basis. By 1984, we had been appointed the club's medical officers.

"It is really odd to think in the 1980s there was virtually no medical cover at rugby matches. In those days, sports medicine was in its infancy. There weren't trained physiotherapists at games. There were just sponge men.

"Remember, these were amateur players in those days. Players just didn't want to stop playing. They would play on until they couldn't do it anymore. If they were injured seriously, these people would lose work. I became involved, with Roger, to try to put some science into it."

Through his direct link with one of rugby's most famous clubs and expertise in developing pioneering knee surgery, Professor Fairclough was as well qualified as anyone to chronicle how rugby's injury problems escalated to crisis level after the game turned professional in 1995.

"Injuries back in the 1980s were relatively minor compared to the modern era," he told me. "Knee and ankle injuries did occur but not that frequently. The injuries tended to be cuts and bruises and minor fractures. There didn't seem to be the big impact injuries you see now."

Neither was concussion considered a major issue. If a player was left dazed, they would slap a wet sponge on his face to revive him and he would just carry on playing.

"In those early days, once in every two games somebody would come off the field with a cut that needed treatment. But they were not that common. By and large back then you would have a small playing squad and you'd be able to play more or less the same people the following week.

"You did have the odd game when there was carnage. I remember a game played against Bridgend at the Brewery Field when there were a lot of fists and boots flying around, but interestingly enough the injuries were all cuts. I can't remember seeing much of the match as we were running out of suture kits putting stitches on players. There were no blood substitutes in those days. We just got players back on the field as soon as we could.

"The first injury of any seriousness I can remember came after we had been covering Cardiff for three or four years. The Wales centre Mark Ring, who originally played fly-half, was probably the most skilful player after Barry John I've ever seen. He was playing against Swansea and he badly damaged his anterior cruciate ligament, needing surgery. It was the first reconstruction we did for a Cardiff player."

It was just a few years into the sport's professional era that Professor Fairclough experienced the worst rugby injury he witnessed first-hand. On a numbing day for Welsh rugby, in December 1997 at Cardiff Arms Park, Fairclough and his friend Dr Evans placed Wales captain Gwyn Jones in a neck brace after he suffered spinal injuries as a result of a double tackle. Later in the same game, Swansea hooker Garin Jenkins, hearing his mother's anguished cry, scaled the perimeter railings to get into the crowd to find his father had suffered a major heart attack, that led to his death a year later. Fortunately, Gwyn Jones recovered from the injury that could have broken his neck but he never played rugby again.

After the game went professional in 1995, rugby changed. "The injury numbers started to become serious in the late 1990s because of the changes to the rules and the advent of professionalism," said Professor Fairclough. "Probably in the first part of the 2000s clubs found they could never field the same team for two games in a row. We did a survey where we showed that at least two players in a team could not play two games running.

"People started to become bigger, they started to become fitter. Then strength and conditioning came in. Because they didn't have to be at work, that led to a completely different individual playing rugby. Players were becoming more physical. It gradually reached the stage where you were no longer dealing with a ball sport, you were dealing with people in a physical confrontation in which the ball was a part.

"As players got bigger and bigger, we started to see more and more different injuries, more upper limb injuries, more dislocated shoulders. Medial injuries to the knees increased, because there were many more tackles. If you are seeing 20 phases, well that's 20 tackles, often with three or four players involved in the breakdown. In each of those tackles, energy is expended which the body has to absorb."

Professor Fairclough wanted to see the body mass index of players being reduced, making them less bulky, so they had the kind of fitness which enabled them to play a full 80-minute match.

"By nature you will remove your Billy Vunipolas because someone 1.88m (6ft 2in) tall, weighing 130kg (20st 6lb) won't last 80 minutes running around the field. They would have to become more athletic, losing weight and power.

"We gradually reached the stage where people were coming on not for injuries but because players could not last for 80 minutes. To me this is exactly analogous with running a marathon and when you reach the 20-mile mark, you get someone to finish the last six.

"You cannot have a situation in which you have two unequal people contesting at the end of a rugby match. If you have a guy who has not been playing for 60 minutes playing against a guy who has been playing for 60 minutes and is very tired, it is an unreasonable physical competition that's not fair. It isn't sport. I don't think it should happen. We know there are more injuries in the second half. Because people get tired, they are more subject to injury. If you bring on fresh impact players, those on the field who started the game are even more prone to being injured.

"If you look at rugby league players, they are physical specimens but they are not huge. Why? Because they have got to last 80 minutes. Look at someone like the French centre Mathieu Bastareaud, who is 1.85m tall (6ft) and weighs 120 kg (19st). He wouldn't last two minutes at rugby league, he's not fit enough. If you have to play for 80 minutes, you cannot carry all that weight around. To say 'impact subs' is a horrific commentary on the sport. I know they mean the person will have an impact [on the game] but they also mean the player will have a literal impact, hurting other people in the tackle. That is not the spirit of the sport I grew up with, where the objective was to get the ball across the try line by going around people with skill and pace."

In November 2013, Professor Fairclough, in an interview

with *The Rugby Paper* as the game's injury crisis deepened, gave his verdict on modern rugby, with this apocalyptic warning: "The human body is not meant to take that amount of force."

The cocktail of circumstances that transformed rugby from being a physical sport to an unacceptably confrontational one goes far beyond just the tackle. As Professor Fairclough pointed out: "Clearing someone out, you are hitting someone who hasn't even got the ball. That I find bizarre."

The fixtures overload players were expected to endure was another reality adding to players being more susceptible to injury. And training, with its aim of trying to harden up players by replicating match conditions, was far from being an injury-free zone. In the study of Welsh professional rugby over a four-year period, Cardiff-based sports medicine specialist Dr Izzy Moore and her team of colleagues found 367 players (86%) in a total player pool of 429 sustained at least one injury during the surveillance period. And 514 of the 2,441 injuries came in training.

Huge players may have posed a daunting-looking problem for smaller players in the contact area, but they themselves were far from immune from injury as opposition players hauled them down. Carrying a large amount of weight can put extra pressure on your joints. The gruesome injury toll suffered by England's powerful world class No 8 Billy Vunipola showed anyone can suffer injury.

In October 2018, he again required surgery after he broke an arm for the third time in 10 months in a torrid battle playing for Saracens against Glasgow Warriors. This meant he missed England's November internationals, adding to a horrendous run of luck that had seen him struggle with shoulder, knee and arm injuries over a two-year period that cost him numerous England Test caps and a place on the 2017 Lions tour to New Zealand.

With disarming honesty, Vunipola, talking to BBC Radio 5 Live in September 2017, tellingly described the burden facing leading rugby players: "I didn't enjoy being on the surgery table twice in one year and that's supposed to be deemed as normal. It gets to a point when you are just done, and you can't control when your knee goes out or your shoulder comes out. That was the weirdest feeling I've ever had in my life, not being able to control that and prevent it from happening. So, something probably needs to change or the players will just burn out."

Professor Fairclough explained: "Billy Vunipola may be bigger and fitter than me but his knee will give way exactly the same."

The huge Welsh centre Jamie Roberts was another vivid example of the injury battles facing even rugby's biggest players. At 1.93m (6ft 4in) and 110kg (17st 5lb), Roberts was bulkier than any Lions player, back or forward, from the famous 1971 tour of New Zealand. None of the players on that triumphant, historic tour weighed as much as 17 stone, while the 23-year-old Scottish lock Gordon Brown, at 6ft 5in, was the only player taller than Roberts.

A qualified doctor, Roberts had no illusions about the game's physical toll saying: "The physio room has resembled a bit of a morgue at times. There are not many who get through their whole career without having to have an operation. I think you're only 100% fit in your first game of rugby."

A successful British & Irish Lion, Roberts was capped 94 times by Wales but paid a heavy price for spending a significant part of his demanding rugby career being used as a battering ram, running into opponents to create phase ball for his side.

"The more games you play, the less time you have to recover," said Professor Fairclough, who witnessed the powerful Roberts lift up a sheep with one arm. "In the long term it will be impossible for Jamie Roberts to have a normal body structure as he has had so many injuries playing rugby. Inevitably he will suffer degenerative arthritis."

The changing face of rugby, with television money and sponsors transforming the game's finances, was symbolised by the disastrous 2005 British & Irish Lions tour in which the tourists suffered a humiliating 3–0 series defeat, being beaten by 18 points or more in every Test by the All Blacks. Sir Clive Woodward, unquestioned as a master coach after his 2003 England World Cup triumph, was allowed to take an army of 30 back-up staff – which included a team of 10 assistant coaches as well as Labour Prime Minister Tony Blair's former spin-doctor Alastair Campbell handling press relations – to support the 48-player tour party, who were playing 11 matches. By contrast, the 1971 Lions had a single coach, the legendary Carwyn James, and their 33-man squad played 26 matches.

"When I first started, the only coach you had was the one taking you to the game," quipped Fairclough. "The last time Roger and I were together at a Cardiff match in 2018, we went down to Lyon in France and there was the main coach, a lineout coach, a fitness coach and I think we counted five physiotherapists. They had their own form of transport because there was no room in the team coach. I am not saying it was wrong – it was a different attitude. The club doctor was no longer the match doctor, he went with the team all the time."

A quietly spoken, affable man, Professor Fairclough looked at serious issues from a scientific, analytical, evidence-based perspective and also retained a flair for the entertaining anecdote. Fairclough's actress daughter earned top marks for initiative gaining a place at Central Saint Martins in London as a drama student when after being told there were no course vacancies she announced: "I'm applying as an international student – I'm from Wales." His memory of leaving the Millennium Stadium with Max Boyce after Wales had been hammered by the old foe from the other side of the Severn is also worth recalling. Giving his verdict on the game, the Welsh balladeer remarked: "I thought England were going to declare at half-time."

Fairclough's call for radical changes to end the game's injury crisis was backed by Dr Izzy Moore, a lecturer at the Cardiff

School of Sport and Health Sciences. Interviewed in August 2018, she said the law changes made by World Rugby "don't seem to be having large impacts". And she echoed Fairclough's concerns about the future of the game, warning: "You might end up in a situation where you have fewer players coming through the system because of the fears of the injury risk."

A study of the game's injury crisis she helped supervise, published in March 2018, examined an injury database covering professional rugby in Wales spanning four years from the 2012–13 season to 2015–16. It confirmed the unhappy situation facing leading players. The study found that the game's concussion problem had increased year-on-year and "on average a professional rugby player was more likely than not to sustain a concussion after 25 matches." It recommended limiting the number of matches played by players in a season to 25, a number far exceeded by leading English players with their heavy club and country commitments.

Its other major finding backed previous studies, stating subsequent injury risk for concussed players was 38% higher than that for players who had not sustained that particular injury. This illustrated the complexity of the sports injury field. The reasons for this worrying statistic had not been unearthed. Were players being returned to action too soon? Or did concussion have a permanent physical or psychological effect, reducing the effectiveness of a player's performance?

Professor Fairclough feels playing rugby became too much of a hazard for players and this was reflected in the declining number of amateur player numbers in Wales.

"When you look at the evidence, the number of people who are actually coming into the game is reducing," he said.

"Specifically, in certain rugby clubs they cannot produce youth teams running up to the age of 18. You still get schools playing rugby but many schools are switching to soccer as it is easier to play, there are less injuries.

"The whole game at professional level has changed. If

you are a small individual you wouldn't consider playing rugby now. No matter what individuals say, the game isn't an attractive proposition. It isn't attractive because it produces too much damage. If I am 5ft 8in tall, would I want to run into someone who is 6ft 4in weighing 20 stone? There are many other sporting avenues which don't injure you so easily."

John Fairclough was a firm believer that the key to rugby's road to redemption lay with returning the sport to a 15-player game with a substitutes bench only used to field replacements for injured players.

"The fundamental priority, as a doctor, is what you need to have is less injures that are caused by impact. If players have to last 80 minutes their body shape has to be different, compared to impact players. If you have a player with less body mass then you will get less serious injuries. The rule changes which have permitted lifting and impact substitutions have meant that people who cannot jump effectively in the lineouts or last 80 minutes can now play rugby. That means they are not the individuals that were playing the game before these changes came in.

"The whole structure of the game will alter if you return rugby to being a 15-man game. Like dominoes, you move one and everything moves. To do that, you have to have an effective criteria for injury assessment. On a number of occasions I've seen uncontested scrums after people have been conveniently injured. But the fact people can cheat is not a reason to suggest the rule change is wrong."

He felt match injuries should be judged by an independent doctor or surgeon. "If I am employed by the club, there is a potential conflict of interest. The decision to play is much more controlled by what the management wants rather than the needs of the player. Match injuries should be assessed by an independent doctor who has the say-so as to whether a person does or does not play.

"When a physiotherapist runs on, you see them trying to

manipulate a shoulder or a leg. You cannot assess the severity of an injury on the pitch. If they are injured, they don't get better by playing on. The role of a physio should be subservient to someone trained in sports science and medicine, who should have the say-so as to whether that person does or does not play.

"If World Rugby's CEO Brett Gosper and chairman Sir Bill Beaumont are saying 'no' to returning rugby as a 15-man sport, please can they justify what improvement they consider impact substitutions have had? If you can't show how they have benefitted the game and they have had a detrimental effect, it should be stopped. World Rugby should be assessing itself, saying 'what can we actually do to make this game safer, reduce the number of injuries and also still make it marketable?' And that has to be looking at keeping people on the field who are equivalently tired and hopefully able to pursue that game for 80 minutes.

"I cannot see a reason why impact subs were introduced in the first place and I cannot see a reason why they should not be ended. They add to the costs of rugby clubs who have to have bigger squads, more coaches and more medical staff and they cause more injuries. They also make the game more complex, deterring newcomers from taking an interest in the sport. I don't see any benefits."

One of the mysteries with rugby injuries spiralling out of control in the 21st century was why World Rugby failed to take the obvious route to making the game safer with more athletic players, by simply restoring rugby's heritage as a 15-man sport with no impact subs. The game was never intended to be a 23-man sport.

"You will find many of the people who are in a position of influence in the rugby world won't rock boats," Professor Fairclough told me. "They may have played rugby but they have never actually been a surgeon. I can rock boats as I don't mind."

World Rugby chairman Sir Bill Beaumont, in his avowed determination to make rugby a safer sport, constantly emphasised the need for "evidence-based programmes" to justify change. Professor John Fairclough spent a lifetime analysing and treating rugby injuries from a medical, fact-based perspective as well as playing the game at junior club level. His damning verdict on the way the game was allowed to become too physical was simply summed up by his view: "No one should be going on to a rugby pitch who can't last 80 minutes."

CHAPTER 5

# The Great Divide –
# Union v League

*"Even conversation or discussion with rugby league clubs
meant you could have a lifetime ban."*

RARELY HAS THERE been so bitter a rivalry between two
sports.

It was hugely ironical that after spending a century
ostracising rugby league for being a professional sport, rugby
union not only discarded its much-vaunted amateur heritage
by turning to professionalism in 1995, but also subsequently,
through ill-judged law variations, succumbed to misguidedly
and unintentionally mimicking much of the physicality found
in the 13-man game, resulting in an unprecedented injury
crisis.

By the time it turned professional, union had so much going
for it. Legendary camaraderie and humour united players from
all walks of life – and even from both sides of the divided island
of Ireland – while spectators packed into stadiums for Test
matches. The ingredients were in place for union to take full
advantage of the commercial opportunities professionalism
would bring, but mistakes made by administrators in the
subsequent decades undermined some of union's great
strengths and introduced new weaknesses.

To understand the relationship between the two codes
and what proved to be its hugely significant implications for

the union game in the modern era, we need to understand the unhappy divisions that existed between the two sports dating back to the Victorian era. In 1895, English rugby union underwent a schismatic crisis when clubs in the north, in a dispute over money, broke away and formed the Northern Union, creating what became rugby league.

In an article published in the *Independent* on 1 May 1999, the award-winning actor/screenwriter Colin Welland (1934–2015), true to his northern roots, wrote, "Rugby league was forged on the anvil of Victorian snobbery." This statement was no exaggeration. Founded at Rugby School in Warwickshire, the setting for Thomas Hughes's celebrated novel *Tom Brown's Schoolday*s published in 1857, rugby union was essentially a product of the public school system. The fact that rugby became popular in great northern industrial towns in Lancashire and Yorkshire proved a cause for concern for those controlling the game, as they worried that its amateur status was being endangered by working-class teams becoming proficient at the sport created by their "social superiors". The glorious chance for rugby union to be a class unifier, rising above the huge wealth and educational divisions found in Victorian England, was sadly lost, to the game's detriment, for the northern clubs were providing a high proportion of the sport's outstanding players.

Payment of any kind was deemed a taint on amateurism in rugby while, by contrast, with the arrival of international sport in the latter part of the 19th century, you could find amateurs and professionals playing alongside each other representing their country in the England cricket team. The greatest sportsman of the Victorian era, WG Grace, a doctor from Gloucestershire revered as "the Father of Cricket", was hardly concerned that, despite being an amateur, he earned more money from England's summer sport than any of his professional fellow players, due to his vast popularity.

The determination of the rugby establishment to turn the

sport into a class battle was summed up by Yorkshire's Harry Garnett, who became RFU president in 1889, when he declared: "If working men desired to play [rugby] football, they should pay for it themselves, as they would have to do with any other pastime."

It need not have been so. Gifted administrator James Miller, a science teacher who had played rugby for Yorkshire, spearheaded the northern movement for reform by proposing players, who lost wages through taking time off work from the great manufacturing centres to play rugby on Saturdays, should be compensated with what became known as "broken time" payments. But in September 1893, the RFU's annual meeting at the Westminster Palace Hotel in London rejected Miller's totally reasonable plea for change, voting down a proposal for broken time payments by 282 to 136 votes.

The inevitable followed on 29 August 1895 at the George Hotel in Huddersfield, when 22 northern clubs effectively gave birth to rugby league, forming the Northern Rugby Football Union and approving "payment for bona fide broken time only".

In Australia, a similar scenario was repeated with more far-reaching consequences, as league would eventually far outstrip the union code in popularity. (In 2013, league players at all levels totalled 1,430,367 in Australia, compared to 323,115 union participants.) The split came in 1907 after the official medical insurance scheme for players was discontinued. This made little sense, for the sport attracted vast crowds. In July 1907, 52,000 watched the All Blacks beat New South Wales 11–3 at the Sydney Cricket Ground.

What followed the creation of rugby league in England was a century of unhappy rivalry between the amateur and professional codes played with the same shaped ball but significantly different laws. Rugby union administrators showed sheer vindictiveness towards players deserting the amateur ranks, banning them from even returning to union

71

clubhouses. In 1930, James Baxter, manager of the Lions for the tour of New Zealand, produced the ultimate example of the contemptuous attitude of the RFU hierarchy when told league was growing in popularity in Auckland by replying: "Every town must have its sewer."

The absurdity of the amateur game's attitude towards the 13-man code was cruelly highlighted in 1933 when Bristol and England full-back Tom Brown travelled north for discussions with a rugby league club. After declining their offer, he accepted a cheque for his travelling expenses and was banned for life from union. He had never played rugby league and only saw the game for the first time when he bought a television set in 1954. In 1987 he was reinstated as an amateur, a gesture of no great consequence as he had died 26 years earlier.

Time failed to bring a more enlightened attitude. The legendary Wales and Lions scrum-half Sir Gareth Edwards, who retired from rugby in 1978, highlighted the witch-hunt atmosphere, recalling: "There was a tremendous amount of stigma attached to rugby league, which made you petrified you were even going to be approached [by league officials] because even conversation or discussion with rugby league clubs meant you could have a lifetime ban."

As late as December 1994, Cambridge University rugby union Blue Ady Spencer was banned after playing eight league games for the London Crusaders before concentrating on his university studies. After explaining to RFU secretary Dudley Wood he had never played league for money, he received the patronising reply: "I really have nothing to add to my previous letter."

By that time, there had been question marks for a number of years over how truly amateur many rugby union players actually were. Rumours abounded about the "boot money" leading players at the major Welsh clubs were given, while being a Welsh rugby star was a route to a decent job for some. There were hints of similar goings-on at some English clubs, however, whatever financial rewards amateur union players ended up with in Britain were pocket money compared with what could be earned by moving north. In 1967, Dai Watkins, the mercurial Newport, Wales and Lions fly-half, joined Salford for a record £15,000, more than 11 times the average yearly salary in the UK at that time.

In England, rugby union, for the most part, retained its elitist image. Before a Twickenham international, the social elite gathered in the West Car Park where hundreds of cars with their open boots produced hampers laden with impressive arrays of fine food and drink, often laid out on trestle tables. Ironically it was a former Rugby School pupil who produced a less flattering description of this scene. The late Philip Toynbee (1916–1981), an Oxford-educated left wing intellectual, said of this giant picnic area: "A bomb under the West Car Park at Twickenham on an International day would end fascism in England for a decade."

Toynbee was by no means the only critic who accused England rugby supporters of being elitist, but, like most generalisations, this was far from the whole story. You wouldn't find the majority of Twickenham spectators in the West Car Park. Most of the crowd descended on the ground by train and Tube with a vast throng flooding the pavements and stopping off for traditional pre-match meets in one of the many local pubs, crowded with rugby followers. Before corporate hospitality, if you wanted to get to the game invariably you could find a party of rugby friends with a spare ticket, as someone had failed to make a rendezvous at The White Cross Hotel, a marvellous 19th-century riverside inn picturesquely placed near Richmond Bridge, the oldest surviving bridge crossing the Thames. And no one would dream of charging a fellow rugby man a penny more than the price of the ticket.

The good-natured pre-match atmosphere was translated to the ground. Most of the crowd at Twickenham on international day would have failed a breathalyser test but there was never a need to separate rival supporters. While an English crowd might never match the inspirational sound nor the expertise of the Welsh choral legions at Cardiff internationals, the Twickenham crowd, in a spontaneous gesture of defiance, drowning out the All Blacks haka by singing England's unofficial anthem 'Swing Low Sweet Chariot' before Will Carling's side defeated New Zealand 15–9 on 27 November 1993 remains a moving memory.

The RFU may have seemed too often in a world of their own, but they deserved credit for expanding the game. Former RFU secretary Dudley Wood, previously an ICI overseas manager, may have been a staunch defender of amateurism but he played a key role in modernising Twickenham's facilities in his ten years working for an organisation which had an ex-directory phone number when he took up the post. Neither was he without a sense of humour, remarking in 1988: "The relationship between the Welsh and the English is based on trust and understanding. They don't trust us and we don't understand them."

While English rugby has primarily been played by the professional classes, labelling it an Establishment sport, entirely peopled by former public schoolboys and Home Counties characters is somewhat wide of the mark. With the creation of rugby league, the RFU lost the north as a major source of talented players, but there was a strong rugby tradition in the West Country with clubs such as Bristol, Bath and Gloucester, and the Midlands where Coventry, Leicester and Northampton could be found.

Throughout the decades, right into the 21st century, the impressive level of good-humoured camaraderie among those actually playing the game made class differences irrelevant. Take the case of two Jasons, who showed a working-class background is not an insurmountable barrier to achieving English rugby's highest honours. In 2005, former rugby league international Jason Robinson, brought up by his Scottish single mother after his Jamaican father left their Leeds home before he was born, became the first mixed-race player to captain England, leading his country against Wales at the Millennium Stadium. In 2015, Jason Leonard, the popular 'Cockney carpenter' who found fame while winning a record 114 England caps in the game's engine room as a prop forward, became the RFU president.

On Lions tours, the Welsh and English buried any differences they had. As the much-revered Welsh fly-half Dai Watkins remarked after captaining the 1966 Lions in New Zealand: "It was even bloody marvellous playing alongside the English." On the 1971 Lions tour in New Zealand, scrum-half Chico Hopkins from Maesteg in the Welsh Valleys and Bob Hiller, the urbane Oxford-educated Harlequins full-back from the opposite end of the social spectrum, formed a memorable double act, entertaining their fellow tourists.

Ireland provide the ultimate example of the sporting brotherhood evoked by the game of rugby union. The Irish rugby team is unusual, as it represents a united Ireland – but it did not entirely escape the consequences of The Troubles, when the IRA used the bullet and the bomb in its bloody campaign seeking a united Ireland, free of British rule. In 1972, 100 British soldiers were killed and 500 injured and Wales and Scotland decided not to play their Five Nations games in Dublin that year as it was deemed too dangerous. In this incendiary atmosphere, few expected England to travel to Dublin the next time they were scheduled to play but led by John Pullin they crossed the Irish Sea in February 1973.

When the English players ran onto the field at Lansdowne Road, the 50,000 crowd rose to their feet, clapping and cheering. England were humbled 18–9 in the match itself but speaking at the after-match dinner, Pullin, a Gloucestershire farmer with a hugely impressive rugby CV, guaranteed himself a place in rugby folklore quipping: "Well we may not be much good but at least we turn up."

Perhaps the most erudite tribute to the virtues of union came from New Zealand's Chief Justice Sir Richard Wild in his speech marking the 75th anniversary of New Zealand rugby in 1967 when he stated: "It's the team element which provides a spur to the weaker spirit, a curb for the selfish and discipline for all. It treats every man as equal from whatever background he comes. There's no yielding to status in a rugby tackle, there's no privilege in a scrum."

But while players made rugby union a great amateur sport, where enjoyment rather than commercialism was the main priority, those controlling the game had much to answer for – and not only for their vitriolic attitude towards rugby league. Until the Anti-Apartheid Movement effectively ended sporting ties with South Africa, rugby ignored the blatant injustices and increasing bloodshed caused by racial segregation in a republic ruled by the white man. The chief culprits were the All Blacks as they were prepared to drop native New Zealanders, the Maoris, from their side when touring South Africa to play their great rivals.

After apartheid ended and Nelson Mandela was elected South African president in April 1994, a new era for rugby was signalled by the huge success of the 1995 World Cup, hosted by the republic. On 24 June 1995, the Springboks defeated the much-vaunted favourites New Zealand, containing the phenomenal Jonah Lomu in their ranks, 15–12 in the World Cup final at Ellis Park, Johannesburg, watched by 60,000 spectators, including President Mandela wearing a Springbok jersey.

Two months later, on 27 August 1995, the International Rugby Board finally ended a century's vendetta against rugby league, announcing rugby union had become an open sport, enabling top-flight players to become professionals. Few could have predicted how much this decision was going to change the game.

The 1995 entry into professionalism was to have far-reaching consequences for rugby union as the 15-man code, largely to its detriment, sought to match the fluency of the 13-man game. However, initially the final abandonment of amateurism merely resulted in a new-found atmosphere of reconciliation, producing cross-code matches. Rugby's Cold War had finally ended after a century and any doubts about the quality of professional league players were soon dispelled on 8 May 1996, in Manchester, when the great Wigan club outclassed Bath, the leading English rugby union club, 82–6 playing the 13-man code, with Martin Offiah, arguably the world's fastest rugby player, running in six tries.

In the return match on 25 May, played under union rules, Bath used their power in the scrum and lineout expertise to record a 41–19 victory watched by 42,000 at Twickenham, but the superb fitness and handling skills of the league side saw them run in two inspirational tries from behind their own line to claim a respectable final scoreline.

In between these two contests, Wigan, captained by the future Wales rugby union defensive coach Shaun Edwards, with speedsters like Offiah and the young Jason Robinson in their ranks, hijacked rugby union's end-of-season festival,outclassing Wasps 38–15 in the Middlesex Sevens final.

With these cross-code encounters signalling the end of outright hostilities, Rugby Football League chief executive Maurice Lindsay predicted the two codes would come together within five years. This didn't turn out to be true, and neither did the prediction from Leicester Tigers chief executive Peter Wheeler, in 2001, that some top league clubs would join the Premiership. His viewpoint was rather an insult to the north's major rugby league towns where even soccer couldn't compete with the passionate support for the 13-man code. There was no way rugby league would surrender its proud heritage and switch to a form of rugby which they regarded as over complex and slow paced.

It was not only rugby administrators producing misguided

predictions. The *Daily Express* newspaper, after Wigan's Sevens triumph, pronounced the league players were "light-years ahead in skill, fitness and technique than anything the union world can offer. Now they are being paid up to £150,000 a year, they [union players] cannot afford to serve up a game where the ball is in play for less than 20 minutes. In league it is often in play for more than 70 minutes." Rugby union administrators did indeed misguidedly seek to produce more ball-in-play time, with damaging consequences. Initially, though, the main consequence of professionalism and the thaw of relations between the two codes involved the interchange of small numbers of major players and coaches.

An impressive list of former rugby union players, such as Welshmen Lewis Jones, Billy Boston, Clive Sullivan, Dai Watkins, Maurice Richards and Jonathan Davies, plus Englishman Martin Offiah, had ranked among the greatest rugby league players in the second half of the 20th century. But the crossover trend was reversed after 1995 and a succession of stars from the northern league clubs switched codes, seeking the higher financial rewards and greater limelight available in the 15-man game.

The league game boasted some wonderful athletes. England could well have won the 1991 union World Cup if they had had the great Wigan trio Ellery Hanley, Shaun Edwards and Martin Offiah playing for them. However, despite all their physical attributes, league stars changing codes in Britain after 1995 found rugby union a far more complex game, with its scrums and lineouts and the fact that play continued after successful tackles.

Wigan winger Jason 'Billy Whizz' Robinson made the leap in style and proved one of the most lethal runners in rugby union history, scoring the crucial try for England in their defeat of Australia in the 2003 World Cup final in Sydney. Another former Wigan back, Chris Ashton, also had a hugely successful England union career as a wing through his outstanding finishing ability, marked by his controversial 'Ash Splash' try-scoring dive, before loss of form and defensive weaknesses saw him dropped after scoring 19 tries in 39 Tests.

But other league stars found it hard to match expectations. It was the disastrous attempt to fast-track Sam Burgess into the England side for the 2015 World Cup that showed the skills in the two codes of rugby were not easily interchangeable. In a spectacular cross-code raid, Bath and the RFU recruited the 25-year-old league superstar – a giant of a man standing 1.96m (6ft 5in) tall and weighing 116kg (18st 4lb). However, he returned to league just a year into his three-year contract. England coach Stuart Lancaster had opted to play this powerful rugby league forward at centre and, having been raced into the team with indecent haste, Burgess struggled as England exited the World Cup at the group stage.

With more experience of understanding the complexities of union forward play, Burgess might have been an outstanding back row forward, but he didn't get that chance. He made his Test debut for England when France were beaten 19–14 in a warm-up match for the 2015 World Cup at Twickenham. Watching from a seat ideally placed just above ground level in the East Stand facing the halfway line, it was obvious to me Burgess had been miscast. True, his shuddering rugby league style high tackles were an intimidating sight. But he had none of the qualities – handling skills, evasiveness, kicking ability or pace – found to some degree in the DNA of an outstanding international union back. This reality could hardly be blamed on his rugby league background. In the same World Cup, Sonny Bill Williams, another physically huge cross-code convert, also playing centre, proved a key player with his masterful offloading ability in the great New Zealand side which defeated Australia 37–17 in the final on 31 October, at Twickenham.

League stars weren't always a success as union players, but league men have had a huge coaching influence in the union game, through the skills gained by operating in a sport where players span the width of the field directly opposing each other, in contrast to the union game where scrums and lineouts could give backs more space.

Phil Larder was the acknowledged mastermind behind England's 2003 World Cup winning defence, while Shaun Edwards, with Wales, and Andy Farrell, with Ireland and the 2013 and 2017 British & Irish Lions, have also proved impressively successful defensive coaches in the 15-man game.

Star league players and coaches found the lure of the union game irresistible, but union administrators mistakenly felt the need to copy league's fluidity in the new professional era, where financial success would be equated with popularity. Quite why the difference between the two codes was perceived as a problem by union administrators was another matter, for times had much changed since the early post-war era when rugby league in England experienced what was an unprecedented boom.

In the 1948–49 and 1949–50 seasons, league spectator numbers reached 6.8 million. In 1954, the Challenge Cup replay featuring Warrington v Halifax at the Odsal Stadium in Bradford recorded a vast official attendance of 102,569. The game's television popularity in the 1960s and 1970s owed much to the fact it was a rare live televised team sport and, also, the cult status of commentator Eddie Waring (1910–86), whose appeal lay in his disarmingly frank narration of what was happening on the field of play allied to a strong Yorkshire accent that southerners found a source of amusement, and catchphrases like "It's an oop n under" and "Ee's gone for an early bath".

Meanwhile, rugby union wasn't concerned about league's television appeal, and proudly claimed that it was a sport for players – evidenced by the fact clubs often ran as many as half a dozen sides. Leading English clubs generally attracted small gates numbering no more than hundreds, but clubhouses at all levels provided a thriving social scene with heavy drinking and boisterous singing sessions in customary post-match rituals more akin to university rag week antics than serious sport.

Writer Michael Green's best-selling book *The Art of Coarse Rugby*, first published in 1960, offered a far-fetched insight into the good-humoured camaraderie. In his catalogue of imaginative acts of gamesmanship, pranks and misdeeds, the coarse rugby player emerged as a man not over-concerned with the athletic aspects of the game. His advice was unequivocal for those spending Saturday afternoons playing in the lower realms of the sport: "Do Not Indulge In A Warm-Up. Countless games are lost because of this foolish habit. It is impossible to exaggerate the boost the other side receive from seeing their opponents throwing the ball to each other and dropping it, taking kicks at goal and missing or doing all-out sprints at walking pace."

Green's insights into the characteristics of Welsh rugby players his coarse player met on tour also deserved noting: "Only one player in the home side could not sing like an opera star and he played the spoons ... I don't think I've ever met a Welshman who hasn't had at least a trial for the national schools' team ... It is not necessarily the ambition of every Welsh player to go north but it is certainly his ambition to say he refused an offer."

This kind of humour has always been a key component of union at all levels, with the divide between forwards and backs being a particularly popular subject for jokes. The Australian lock, Peter FitzSimons, capped seven times in 1989–1990, stated: "Rugby backs can be identified because they generally have clean jerseys and identifiable partings in their hair. Come the revolution the backs will be the first to be lined up against the wall and shot for living parasitically off the work of others."

The fact that rugby union's playing fraternity in the amateur era featured people from all walks of life and with

81

vastly different personalities was another of its great strengths. There is no shortage of stories about high jinks and downright thuggery among the forwards of the era, but recall the career of the late Jackie Kyle (1926–2014), the Ireland and Lions fly-half genius in the early post-war years, and you are a world away from the dark arts of forward play. A literate, modest, quietly religious man who took the *Rubaiyat of Omar Khayyam* as reading matter on the 1950 Lions tour to New Zealand, Kyle later ignored the option of a successful career as a Belfast surgeon, becoming a medical missionary instead. Asked about his three decades caring for the sick in Zambia's Copperbelt, Kyle replied: "I was only the second opinion. They always saw the witch doctor before me."

While rugby league attracted huge television audiences in the post-war era, rugby union's main spectator appeal lay with international matches, which were great social occasions and invariably attracted full houses. There was heavy demand for tickets for the annual International Championship (later the Five Nations, now the Six Nations) and that was matched by huge interest in the Tests played against the formidable New Zealand and South African rugby giants embarking on major tours of the UK and France.

The popularity of the rugby union tour can be traced back to the startling success of the first two New Zealand tours of Britain and France, when the All Blacks featured an impressive array of great backs in their ranks. Christened the Originals, the 1905–6 All Blacks sensationally won 34 of their 35 tour matches in Europe, France and Canada, scoring a massive 976 points with a mere 59 scored by their opponents. Only Wales, with their historic 3–0 victory at Cardiff Arms Park, were able to defeat the visitors. Later came the 1924–25 All Blacks, the Invincibles, winning all their 32 matches.

South Africa, with their emphasis on forward domination, failed to match the early All Blacks as entertainers but there was a huge interest factor in seeing if these feared tourists could be beaten. Their Test record was even better than that of their great southern hemisphere rivals. While New Zealand lost three of the first four Tests they played against Wales from 1905 to 1953 and were beaten 13–0 by England on their 1935–36 tour, the only Test defeat suffered by South Africa in a sequence of 24 internationals in their first five tours of Europe was Scotland's 6–0 win against the first 1906–7 Springboks, led by Paul Roos. When their 1960–61 tour ended with a 0–0 draw against France, the Springboks had suffered just eight defeats in 147 matches played on those five trips.

However, vast Test crowds failed to obscure just how dreary the game had become in the 1950s and 1960s. For an insight into what a negative spectacle rugby union could produce, just recall the notorious 1963 Murrayfield match when Wales beat Scotland 6–0. In a contest dominated by the kicking skills of the Welsh captain, scrum-half Clive Rowlands, the match featured no less than 111 lineouts. And the New Zealand domination of northern hemisphere nations during the 1960s was briefly halted when Wilson Whineray's 1963–64 tourists drew their match with Scotland 0–0 in Murrayfield, an unthinkable scoreline in rugby's modern era. In the 1958–59 International Championship, England failed to score a try in their four matches and you could be forgiven for thinking you were looking at soccer results with England drawing 3–3 with Scotland at Twickenham, losing 5–0 to Wales at Cardiff, beating Ireland 3–0 in Dublin and drawing 3–3 with France at Twickenham.

It was left to the British & Irish Lions, primed with the best backs produced by the Home Nations, to showcase the sport's potential as an entertainment at that time. In 1955 in South Africa, the Lions, with a buccaneering back line that included Welsh fly-half Cliff Morgan, the hugely gifted England centre Jeff Butterfield and the sensational 19-year-old Irish wing Tony O'Reilly, scored 10 tries, drawing the Test series 2–2. Then the 1959 Lions in New Zealand, containing dazzling backs such as

83

England fly-half Bev Risman, the Irish centre David Hewitt, O'Reilly and the famously elusive Englishman Peter Jackson on the wings and the versatile Scot Ken Scotland at full-back, averaged more than four tries a game. In the infamous first Test, the tourists scored four tries only to be beaten 18–17 as All Blacks full-back Don Clarke landed no less than six penalties.

But the attacking deeds of these Lions teams did no more than provide a spectacular escape from the norm, until a seemingly insignificant event began a transformation of rugby union as a spectacle – a change which really should have encouraged union's administrators at the dawn of the professional era to believe in the strengths of their own sport, rather than make changes to try to match the fluidity of league.

In August 1963, John Dawes, a 23-year-old Welsh teacher from the Valleys, moved to London, simply to give his wife the opportunity to become a professional opera singer, and he joined the London Welsh club at Old Deer Park, in the shadow of the pagoda at Kew Gardens, on the other side of the Thames to Twickenham. After the Exiles suffered a disastrous 1964–65 season, losing 24 of their 36 games, Dawes became club captain and, in six memorable years, turned London Welsh into Europe's most glamorous rugby club. Ignoring the convention that you had to play large forwards, Dawes, in the dual role of club captain and coach, adopted the near-revolutionary yardstick of picking only players with footballing ability. Dubbed 'The Robin Hoods of Rugby', his side, laden with gifted runners who had left Wales to pursue careers in London, amazed everyone, beating major clubs with dazzling back play and a lightweight pack which won little ball but reigned supreme in the loose with fitness and handling skills not normally associated with the men inhabiting the game's engine room.

"When you played against those guys [London Welsh] it was like meeting the Harlem Globetrotters with studs on," was the view of the much-admired Neath and Wales blindside flanker Dai Morris. "They ran everything."

It wasn't until the Exiles had humiliated the strongest Welsh clubs at Old Deer Park, beating Neath 45–3 in February 1968 and then Newport 31–5 in November that same year, that the Welsh selectors finally gave Dawes a full remit, appointing him captain of his country to translate the London Welsh game to the highest level. In a remarkable sequence, Dawes captained Wales to the Grand Slam in 1970–71, then in partnership with the Welsh coaching genius Carwyn James led the 1971 British & Irish Lions to their historic first series victory in New Zealand and finally guided the Barbarians to their famous 23–11 win against Ian Kirkpatrick's All Blacks at Cardiff Arms Park on 27 January 1973.

Two other factors promoted the London Welsh model. In 1967, the All Blacks staged a memorable undefeated tour of Britain and France, playing expansive rugby under their great coach Fred 'the Needle' Allen. A year later, the inspirational Australian Dispensation Law ended the ability to gain ground by kicking into touch from outside the 22, which then encouraged other sides to follow the Dawes running rugby philosophy.

The 1971 Lions heralded the renaissance of British rugby, providing a huge boom in the game's popularity and more importantly, ultimately transformed New Zealand rugby, ending its obsession with forward play after what Graham Henry termed "the biggest wake-up call in New Zealand rugby history". It was no coincidence that Henry and Steve Hansen, the two coaches responsible for the All Blacks winning two successive World Cups in 2011 and 2015, were heavily influenced by witnessing first-hand, as kids in New Zealand, the deeds of the 1971 Lions. Joe Schmidt, the outstanding former Ireland coach, Warren Gatland, successful coach of Wales and the 2013 and 2017 Lions sides, and Vern Cotter, who did much to raise the profile of Scottish rugby, were also youngsters when the 1971 Lions defeated their heroes.

The famous 1971 Lions half-backs and backline were arguably unique for the fact every member – Gareth Edwards, Barry John, David Duckham, Mike Gibson, John Dawes, Gerald Davies and JPR Williams – was a great player. With limited ball, they were relatively subdued in the Test series, but the attacking rugby they played to win all 20 games outside the Tests stunned a rugby nation used to their leading provincial sides regularly humbling touring teams. So great was the public interest, 750,000 spectators in a country with a population of just 2.8 million watched the Lions.

The 47–9 demolition of Wellington at Athletic Park on 5 June 1971, when the Lions scored nine tries against one of the strongest New Zealand provinces, was one of British and Irish rugby's greatest achievements and left the host nation in a state of disbelief. Carwyn James and John Dawes formed one of rugby's greatest partnerships as coach and captain, importantly backed by Scotsman Doug Smith's masterful handling of the tour manager role. Although Carwyn is remembered as the main man who enabled the Lions to attain their Everest, Dawes and his club London Welsh were the key driving force behind British rugby's renaissance. Seven club members were on the 1971 Lions tour and a third of the Test team in all four Tests – Dawes, Gerald Davies, JPR Williams, Mervyn Davies and John Taylor – were Exiles.

Where the Lions had led in 1971, the great Welsh sides of the 1970s followed, providing rugby's equivalent of the Brazilian football teams in terms of excitement. Gone were the Dark Ages of the 1950s and 1960s when rugby union matches were dominated by kicking and rugby results all too often resembled soccer scores.

But, despite the fact union offered so much entertainment for spectators, as well as fun for players, when the game turned professional a couple of decades later, union attempted to become more like league, rather than the other way around. What concerned rugby union administrators was the ball was in play in union matches for as little as 35 minutes 25 seconds in the 1991 World Cup matches, while in rugby league the in-play figure could exceed 60 minutes. But there was no logical reason to make changes in order to improve union's chances of being a commercial success, for league's heyday as a hugely popular televised sport back in the 1960s had long since passed. The 1991 World Cup hosted by England near the end of the game's amateur era attracted average crowds of 31,932, far in excess of the 17,707 average for league's World Cup held in England in 1995.

The advent of professionalism saw the popularity gap between the two codes widen even further, with the expansion of union stadiums, sponsorship and the huge technical advances in television coverage. The 2013 Rugby League World Cup staged by England attracted 458,483 spectators with an average match attendance of 16,071 supporters for the 28 fixtures. By contrast rugby union's 2015 World Cup, also hosted by England, had 2,477,805 spectators watching its 48 games, with the average attendance being 51,620. The total estimated television audience for the league World Cup was 134 million, while the union figure was 120 million for the final alone. The 2017 Rugby League World Cup held in Australia, rugby league's heartland, attracted an average gate of just 13,338 and the host country's 6–0 win playing England in the final, hailed as one of the great league Tests, failed to attract a full house.

In 2018 came a stark reminder that league was a distant second to the union game in popularity. On 4 November 2018, the England rugby league team beat New Zealand 20–14 in an exciting encounter at Anfield. But the series-winning victory was watched by just 26,234 spectators, despite the fact ticket prices were as low as £25. By contrast, the England union team were narrowly beaten 16–15 at Twickenham a week later by the world champions New Zealand, watched by a capacity 82,149 crowd with a huge top ticket price of £195.

For those who championed the far greater fluidity of rugby league, it was worth asking the question why union was the more popular game. League only had a major following in Australia and the north of England (frequent attempts to colonise London had failed) and the game's top tier was inhabited by just three countries, Australia, England and New Zealand, despite being created back in 1895.

Analysing why rugby union became far more popular than rugby league was not a straightforward exercise. Rugby league was far better suited for playing in schools, for without scrums, lineouts and possession battles at the breakdown it was both safer and easier to teach and understand. Also, its greater flow and simplicity was an obvious advantage in attracting newcomers. However, the reality was rugby union, for all its shortcomings as a spectator sport when back play was not a priority, had more appeal. Perhaps the answer lay in its complexity avoiding the repetition of league.

League in its scope could be compared to draughts, where moves are relatively straightforward, while union was more like chess, where the bishops, knights and castles manoeuvre in completely different ways while the queen can move in any direction. The failure of a man hailed as a league superstar, Sam Burgess, when playing union provided a telling example of the failure of rugby union's administrators to appreciate the fundamental differences between the two oval ball codes.

In the 25 years after the game turned professional in 1995, rugby union was run with a worrying degree of the autocratic indifference to criticism which was inherited from the amateur era. Despite its popularity, union failed to escape the shadow of rugby league, with hugely damaging consequences.

# CHAPTER 6

# Farewell Common Sense

*"Why on earth did rugby ever pass regulations which allow more than half the starting team to be replaced? Perhaps idiocies are more obvious with hindsight but idiocy it definitely is."*

WITH RUGBY UNION becoming a Darwinian perversity, with size all too often outweighing skill, World Rugby could have solved the game's injury crisis by simply abandoning the law changes made in the professional era that transformed rugby union from a physical into a dangerous sport. The solutions may have appeared little more than common sense but they required the game's guardians to show a decisiveness, acting for the betterment of the game, that had been sadly lacking.

Well-publicised concerns about giving injured players the best medical attention were all very commendable but their efforts to make the game safer proved lamentably inadequate. It was all very well ensuring a fire is put out effectively, but was it not better to prevent it happening in the first place?

No one wanted to sanitise rugby. But in the 25 years following the decision to pay leading players in 1995, the International Rugby Board/World Rugby, with their endless counter-productive tinkering with the laws and their failure to strictly enforce existing laws sadly eroded the game's heritage as an intriguing and combative struggle for possession between two opposing packs of forwards. Players became hugely impressive tackling machines while sides retained the ball for as many as

20, 30 and even 40 phases. In 2015, a World Rugby study found sides were keeping the ball an average of 13 out of 14 times at the breakdown, nine times out of 10 at the scrum and eight out of 10 in the lineout. The damning reality was the no doubt well-intentioned but misguided efforts to match the flow of the rugby league game to add spectator appeal had made rugby union increasingly physical, predictable and dangerous.

The 15-player game had been facing the same problem league had endured in the post-war era, with sides interminably holding onto the ball, but with more damaging consequences as tackles in the union game produced breakdown collisions while, in league, play was simply halted for a quick restart. Unlike the rival sport, league admistrators had the vision to solve the ball-retention problem. In 1966, Rugby Football League secretary Bill Fallowfield introduced what became the six tackle law, with a possession handover after the sixth tackle. But more than 50 years later, rugby union lawmakers were unwilling to adopt the obvious solutions to end the possession monopoly.

Incredible it may seem but before his unexpected death in 1983, the legendary Welsh coach Carwyn James advocated the simple but crucial law change that would have made rugby in the professional era both less physical and easier to referee.

Prophetically Carwyn James and the late *Daily Telegraph* rugby correspondent John Reason, one of the shrewdest observers of the game's intricacies, in their book *The World of Rugby – A History of Rugby Union Football*, published in 1979 before today's leading players were born, correctly predicted the onset of rugby league style tackling that became a major feature of the union game after a seemingly relatively innocuous law change allowed tackled players to pass the ball provided they managed to keep it off the ground.

They cited the 1978 Wales v France match when Welsh centre Ray Gravell, grounded by a superb Christian Bélascain tackle, passed the ball to Phil Bennett who scored a try writing: "Now if the tackler, in this case Christian Bélascain, is not rewarded with at least an interruption in the attacking side's control of the ball he will soon come to the conclusion that there is no point in him making the classic side-on or head-on tackle at all. He will, instead, stand up and maul for the ball, as they do in rugby league. Is that really what the International Board wants from rugby union football?

"The changes in the tackle law were made to speed up play. They have not succeeded. Instead they have introduced the pile-up, as players seek to keep the ball off the ground and opponents seek to smother it. They have devalued the tackle and they have almost eliminated the ruck.

"The solution is obvious. There must be a return to the old law which required a player immediately to release the ball once he had been brought to the ground. This would give the successful tackler a fair reward. But it would still provide the attacking team with the possibility of recovering possession by a ruck, or a running scrum."

Sadly, the truth proved far worse than even James envisaged. Tackled players being allowed not only to pass but to manhandle the ball on the ground in the professional era resulted in ever-higher tackle and injury counts, as regaining possession at the breakdown became an ever-rarer event. Rather than seeking to evade opponents, players were happy to charge directly into them for phase after phase, knowing that they were unlikely to lose possession.

In his *Guardian* newspaper columns he wrote before his death in 1983, Carwyn James, with visionary accuracy, noted the changing nature of the sport, writing: "This new midfield 'crash-ball' is a disaster – hunks of manhood with madness in their eyes, battering-ram bulldozers happy to be picked off on the gain-line by just-as-large hunks from the opposing side. For what? Just to do it all over again.

"Back play at speed is becoming a pathetic apology, an insult to those who have graced it for a century. Flat-footed forwards now stand at centre: I ask you! We are breeding robots."

In 1998, the late Frank Keating, one of Britain's outstanding sports journalists, in his *Guardian* sports column was found lamenting the influence of the league code on the union game and the increasing importance attached to what he termed "the weights room dungeon", writing: "I went to a rugby union match on Saturday and a rugby league match broke out. It was the so-called friendly between the Welsh champions Swansea and England's Premiership club West Hartlepool but it could well have been Wigan Bulldozers v Widnes Pantechnicons (or whatever they call themselves these days) so utterly single-minded was the scary one-track collision-course game totally relied on by both sides. The overwhelming yardstick now in rugby union is not finesse and charm, daintiness and dexterity with the ball. All is crunch and scrunch, pulverising power.

"Full-time rugby means pro-weightlifters. I am told they are at it noon and night from Harlequins to Hartlepool."

While Keating's verdict, laced with humour, seemed unduly influenced by his unflattering view of rugby league, he did provide anecdotal evidence backing his view that power was replacing skill, including quoting a 17-year-old who had written to *Rugby World* magazine seeking advice on gym training, asking: "If I train with heavy weights, will I lose my speed? But if I do not lift weights then I may not gain strength."

In 2006, John Dawes echoed Carwyn's concerns, telling *Independent* sports writer Brian Viner: "Since professionalism there has been an influx of rugby league influence and I find it unbelievable to see the players lined up across the field. Not a back amongst them. Whereas professionalism has produced bigger, faster, stronger players, it hasn't improved the skill factor at all."

Common sense dictated rugby union needed to end tackled players playing a vital role in enabling their side to keep possession interminably. In the 1991 World Cup, the average match produced 94 tackles. This figure had more than doubled to over 200 in the 2011 World Cup in New Zealand. In the English 2017–18 season, the tackle average had risen by 33.2% since the 2013–14 season.

These figures didn't tell the full story of how much rugby had changed. Especially exasperating was the huge number of blatantly illegal solo charges on players who hadn't even got the ball at the breakdown going unpunished. Occasionally, in extreme cases, players were penalised. When Australia knocked England out of the 2015 World Cup with a 33–13 win at Twickenham, the back row forward Michael Hooper was penalised for a rhino-like shoulder charge, crashing into England full-back Mike Brown who was nowhere near the ball. Hooper was later given a one-match ban for dangerous play.

Then, in the second Test of the British & Irish Lions tour to New Zealand in 2017, prop forward Mako Vunipola was fortunate to just get sin-binned rather than red-carded for charging into the prone All Blacks fly-half Beauden Barrett dangerously close to the New Zealander's head.

Leading British rugby correspondent Brendan Gallagher, writing in *The Rugby Paper* on 31 December 2017, produced a withering indictment of the practice, saying: "Sort out the thuggery at clear-out time, start reffing it properly. The clear out doesn't exist in law and certainly shouldn't be used as an excuse for players who are not bound to launch themselves off their feet like an Exocet and take out-injure-maim players who are behind the ball and legally bound on. Or sometimes just trying to reach the ruck.

"When exactly did that become legal? Did I miss the memo? They have no right to half kill the bloke who has been good enough to get there first and dominate the contact area."

On 27 July 2019 in Wellington, New Zealand, during a compelling Rugby Championship Test between the All Blacks and South Africa that ended in a 16–16 draw, a single incident offered a damning insight into the way World Rugby had mismanaged rugby union, making it a dangerous sport. Spectators witnessed the sad sight of the massive All Blacks lock Brodie Retallick leaving the field after 60 minutes, holding a dislocated shoulder after being floored by a thunderous illegal clear-out charge by the equally huge impact sub, lock forward RG Snyman. The South African wasn't even penalised or later blamed. All the subsequent publicity centred on whether Retallick would make the World Cup.

As Stuart Barnes, reporting the match, wrote in *The Sunday Times:* "Retallick's absence from the World Cup would be a devastating blow for both man and team. Yet, as Retallick left the field in obvious pain, there was no reprimand for the man who did not attempt to follow the laws of the game and bind into another player. Not even a penalty. I don't blame Snyman. He only did what countless 'clear outers' of breakdowns do every week, oblivious to the laws of the game. I don't blame the referee Nic Berry either. To single out the second row would have been a case of scapegoating. Referees have been allowed to give leeway to speed the flow of the game. Yesterday was inevitable. Rather blame World Rugby for failing to clamp down on this ugly aspect."

The Retallick injury was a classic example of the hypocrisy of World Rugby failing to enforce its own laws while CEO Brett Gosper claimed the game was "safer than ever" and chairman Sir Bill Beaumont equally absurdly stated rugby union was a sport "leading the way in injury prevention". The ridiculous situation was, while World Rugby constantly uttered the platitude "player welfare is our No 1 priority", the game's injury crisis made a mockery of this claim.

The "bind" law ensured a degree of safety at the breakdown. So what did World Rugby do? It perversely promoted dangerous play by ensuring elite referees kept the game flowing by ignoring dangerous, illegal no-arms clear-out charges. The result in Wellington: Brodie Retallick was sent crashing to the ground with a dislocated shoulder that jeopardised his participation in the World Cup. Ironically, if Retallick had been holding a rugby ball, Snyman could well have been red-carded for dangerous play. If it had happened in the street, he could have been charged with assault and acquired a criminal record.

For anyone in doubt about the hypocrisy of the situation, in March 2019 England flanker Sam Underhill told *The Rugby Paper*: "At the breakdown the letter of the law is you have to bind. Yet no one binds."

The Wellington Test also offered an interesting insight into the fact the often-repeated observation that the small man no longer had a place on the rugby field was not entirely true. Ironically, after 6ft 7in (2m) 19st (121kg) Retallick left the field injured, the game was drawn with a thrilling last-minute converted try that showed skill could still outplay size in rugby. The score came when the Springboks' speedy 5ft 7in winger Cheslin Kolbe tore down the right flank and his clever chip ahead was gathered by his dynamic scrum-half colleague, 5ft 6in Herschel Jantjies, who had scored two tries during his sensational debut Test playing Australia a week earlier.

The reality was, at the game's top level, modern rugby had become a dangerous sport for everyone, whatever their size. The fact England's most formidable physical players, centre Manu Tuilagi and No 8 Billy Vunipola had been sidelined from Test rugby for years showed even the game's largest players were unable to avoid the injury crisis.

Around the time of the 2015 World Cup, referees were reducing the mayhem at the breakdown and making the game flow better by simply applying existing laws more strictly.

Subsequently, the breakdown contest had been consistently halted after initial collisions with referees announcing, "The ball is available", ending any further competition for possession, and scrum-halves being instructed to "Use it". Quite why they were allowed to go into pose mode for five seconds before obeying this instruction, unhindered by opponents, was another matter.

But clear-out charges remained unpenalised.

The ruck, perfected by the All Black sides in the amateur era as an aesthetically pleasing way of gaining possession, with forwards binding on each other and driving over the ball making it quickly available, had become virtually redundant. How the hell could you ruck the ball effectively with your route forward blocked by the tackled player who had failed to release the ball when hitting the deck and other players who remained sprawled on the ground or rested motionless with knee on the ground forming a barricade, while others knocked over players who hadn't even got the ball in illegal clear-out charges?

Modernists welcomed the end of the ruck, rating it as dangerous. But it was the modern game that featured players regularly departing the field injured, while it was difficult to recall Test matches in the past where a ruck resulted in players having to go off. True, All Black Colin Meads ended the Test career of the great Australian scrum-half Ken Catchpole, famed for his lightning pass, in a ruck situation in 1968. But what Meads did was hardly an act of rucking. Told to stop Catchpole burrowing back into the pack, he recalled: "Sure enough, the little bugger ducked back in amongst us. I just reached in and grabbed one leg. I was going to tip him up. I didn't know his other bloody leg was stuck at an angle. So he did the splits. Bloody sad."

A decade later on 13 December 1978, All Blacks prop John Ashworth twice viciously and deliberately stamped on the face of JPR Williams when the great full-back, playing for Bridgend, was trapped on the side of the ruck. Williams left the field with blood streaming from a hole in his cheek in a game won 17–6 by the tourists. However this was not rucking but a pure act of unpunished thuggery, leaving an opponent needing 30 stitches, and it could well have earned a lifetime ban in the game's professional era.

As Nick Easter, the Harlequins and England No 8, old enough to recall when the ruck was in use, said four years

# Rugby union leaders in denial mode

World Rugby CEO Brett Gosper, a marketing master, who repeated his 2016 claim rugby was "safer than ever" in 2019 after the deaths of four young French players in eight months.

World Rugby chairman Sir Bill Beaumont, who complacently first termed rugby "a leader in sport in the prevention and management of injury" in 2017 with "player welfare" as the main priority despite the game's unacceptable injury levels.

# Two distinct features of rugby's professional era

Breakdown chaos. Who to penalise? Players illegally seeking to control a pile-up during a Scotland v Australia Test.

© Getty Images

Modern rugby's homage to power. The touring All Blacks gym training in November 2018 before facing England at Twickenham.

© Getty Images

# The changing face of the rugby tackle

High tackling duet in rugby's professional era. Rugby league convert Sam Burgess and Owen Farrell committing illegal league-style high tackles during Australia's 33–13 World Cup win at Twickenham on 3 October 2015.

© Getty Images

The traditional amateur era low tackle. Australian fly-half John Ballesty tackling the legendary All Black lock Colin Meads during New Zealand's 27–11 win in Sydney on 15 June 1968. Note the tackler keeping his head out of harm's way.

© Peter Bush / Colorsport

# The demise of the traditional rugby scrum

Parisian scrum fiasco. English referee Wayne Barnes ordering yet another scrum reset at the end of the 100-minute France v Wales Six Nations match on 18 March 2017.

Former England hooker Brian Moore, champion of the traditional rugby scrum, with front row colleagues Victor Ubogu (left) and Jason Leonard (right) and a youthful Martin Johnson in the background ready for battle in Will Carling's successful England side in the 1990s.

# Treating rugby's casualties

Professor John Fairclough and Dr Izzy Moore (below), two Cardiff-based experts on rugby's injury crisis.

Professor Fairclough at the rear of the stretcher party that included fellow Cardiff club medic Dr Roger Evans (in brown jacket) carrying Gwyn Jones off the field at Cardiff Arms Park on 13 December 1997 after carefully treating the severe spinal injury that ended the career of the Wales captain.

# Highs and lows of professional rugby

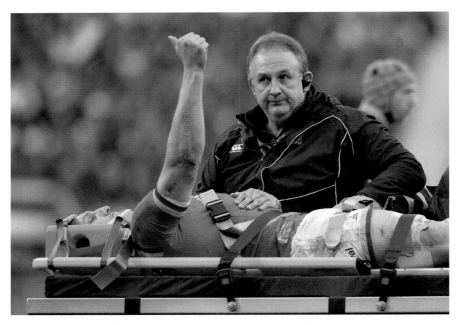

12 March 2016. Yet another concussion victim. Wales captain Sam Warburton tells the crowd he is OK after severe blow to his head playing England at Twickenham.

© Getty Images

29 June 2009. Rugby's Red Army. A shot of the British & Irish Lions supporters on tour duty at the 2nd Test v South Africa at Loftus Versfeld Stadium in Pretoria.

# A major feature of modern rugby was the end of the racism in the sport's amateur era

The legendary Cardiff -born winger Billy Boston, who turned to league to find stardom in the 1950s.

Full-back George Nepia, 19-year-old star of the 1924–25 Invincibles tour of Britain, dropped, as he was a Maori when his country played South Africa.

© Getty Images

A sport for all races. South Africa's captain Siya Kolisi, raised in the townships, receiving the 2019 World Cup from Japan's Crown Prince Akishino.

© Getty Images

# Two rugby visionaries from the Valleys

Master coach Carwyn James with the 1971 Lions. In 1979, he and *Daily Telegraph*'s rugby correspondent, John Reason, cited the key law change ignored by modern rugby administrators, writing: "There must be a return to the old law which required a player immediately to release the ball once he had been brought to the ground."

© Colorsport

Former Wales and Lions captain John Dawes (pictured breaking in the famous 23–11 Barbarians victory versus the 1972–73 All Blacks), lamenting the physicality of modern rugby in 2013, stated: "You would be penalized in our day for a pile-up. But now they just dive in jumping on each other. I can't understand how the referee allows it."

© Colorsport

before he retired in 2016 at the age of 37: "There's a clear difference between rucking and stamping. One involves a backward movement with the boot, the other a downward one. I've always been a fan of rucking. Lord knows why they've outlawed it.

"I've never come across any player anywhere who's against it. In the old days, if there was a body lying on the ball, you'd just give them a bit of shoe to get them out of the way. Simple. Clean. Effective."

A graphic illustration of modern rugby's injury crisis came early in the 2017–18 season when leading English club Wasps suffered an uncharacteristic 9–27 home defeat against Bath at the Ricoh Arena after injuries decimated their squad, leaving them with just 24 fit players for the game.

"In the first ten minutes when we played Exeter in the previous game, we had to defend for 36 phases," recalled phlegmatic, much respected Wasps coach Dai Young. "The game is going very much towards keeping the ball for long periods, more contacts. It's very hard to protect players."

Rugby union's emergence as a dangerous sport with the skill/power balance distorted was no sudden event. For years, the game had been scarred by collapsed scrums and breakdown chaos. In 2013 in Cardiff, two much-admired figures from the world of rugby and medicine produced damning warnings that the game had lost its way, becoming too physical.

In the summer of that year I drove from Birmingham to Llandaff, the suburb on the outskirts of the Welsh capital noted for its cathedral, picturesquely placed in a drop in the landscape, to interview John Dawes, whose achievements leading London Welsh, Wales, the 1971 Lions and 1973 Barbarians had transformed rugby. Brick wall rugby, substitutes galore and endless gym sessions had little appeal for Dawes. During the morning I spent at his home, he provided a quietly spoken, eloquently reasoned, withering indictment of the way rugby had been allowed to change for the worse.

"What the game has developed now is physicality. These days the first thing you look at in a player is how big he is, how strong he is. This is best exemplified by the current Welsh team that has just won the Six Nations – the back division is huge," Dawes said.

"You don't see the ball go down the line from set pieces. When did you last see the top of the lineout ball go straight down the line to the wing?

"When we were playing, the game was for the players, about the players. Now the game is dominated by the coach and his team. If you pass it out to the wing from a set piece, you get into a row with the coach. If you do it twice, you are dropped!

"I don't think Carwyn James ever told me how to play. We just talked. It was just a natural relationship. He was a listener rather than a teller. He would select guys for a particular skill. If they perform that skill you are happy. If they don't, you have to think why. It is a selection rather than a coaching problem.

"These days they don't see a scrum or a lineout as a means of scoring. All the teams have pace but they don't use it. It is not their priority. They move the ball X phases and X phases means physicality You have to have four or five pile-ups before you score a try. What you see is a mess.

"With a ruck, you could see the ball on the floor and the forwards were pushing over it, binding together much like a scrum. A maul was the same except the ball was in the hands. Nowadays it's a pile-up. You would be penalised in our day for a pile-up. But now they just dive in, jumping on each other. I can't understand how the referee allows it.

"I find it sad. What I'd like to see is someone take it on and movement of the ball. I would return to straight put-ins and the ruck and maul as they used to be. The laws haven't changed. They have the same amount of forwards in the scrum, the distance between the threequarter lines is just the same. These days they don't even strike for the ball in the scrums. You don't get one against the head unless a scrum is outshoved.

"The other thing is replacements. The front row battle used to be resolved in the last 20 minutes of a game. There was a degree of pride in who won that battle. But now with substitutes it's a different game.

"Where the game has become a little more dangerous is in the size of people. There is more emphasis on fitness and weight training. Playing physically as they do now, injuries will increase."

A few months later, in November 2013, Professor John Fairclough, who had developed a pioneering knee surgery treatment at the University Hospital of Wales in Cardiff during a lifetime of treating rugby injuries, echoed the views of Dawes that rugby had become too physical. Interviewed by *The Rugby Paper*, he called for change, stating: "The impact at ruck and maul must be reduced. It alarms me totally. This is not Rollerball and yet we talk about 'breaking the line'. You can't go round people now. The game we see now is not the game as it used to be.

"You cannot just clear people out of the ruck, least of all when they're not looking. That means they're not braced for impact and that's where serious knee injuries occur. It was a sport for all shapes and sizes, then it became a sport for freaks. Look at people like Leigh Halfpenny and Shane Williams. They went from being very quick, very lithe and relatively light to having to bulk up. Look at the amount of injury that Leigh in particular has suffered. There is an inevitability that serious injuries will continue to rise. The human body is not meant to take that amount of force."

Also in 2013, the great Ireland and Lions captain Willie John McBride, a giant in every sense of the word, issued a similar warning about the game's undue emphasis on power, telling his audience at an event in Birmingham: "Modern rugby is all about big men bulking up. I know kids of 16 or 17 who are a funny shape. It concerns me."

Sadly, the views of Dawes, Professor Fairclough and McBride had no impact.

Fronted by a dismissively evasive PR department at its Dublin headquarters, World Rugby, through its failure to ensure even its own laws were enforced, left referees negotiating a minefield of illegalities surfacing at scrums and tackle area pile-ups. And players regularly escaped censure for ignoring the offside and obstruction laws in open play.

When we last spoke, in the summer of 2016, Dawes told me he no longer felt he followed the game closely enough to pass judgment. His disillusionment with modern rugby was understandable. In the late 1960s at London Welsh, this was the man who had taken rugby union to a new level by adopting the pioneering concept of picking forwards for their footballing ability above bulk. Ironically, half a century later the game had reverted to size being a major priority not only among forwards but backs too, with many backs being far bigger than the forwards of yesteryear. His philosophy of "let the ball do the work" was all too frequently ignored.

What happened during games was not the only problem. In training, coaches aiming to replicate match conditions were raising injury tolls. It reached the stage where Premiership clubs were questioning the training methods of hard taskmaster England coach Eddie Jones after finding some players returning injured from England squad sessions. With a £24,000 match fee for playing for their country, players were hardly likely to risk questioning training schedules imposed on them.

The situation in training offered an obvious but ignored route to significantly reducing injuries. Playing matches was just part of the life of a professional rugby player, but the majority of their time was spent training, mostly unseen by the general public. Alarmingly, at the game's top level as many as a third of the injuries were quoted as occurring on the training field, with coaches replicating match conditions, trying out tactics and evaluating the ability of players in high contact situations. With their livelihoods at stake, players were in no position to contest coaching methods. But those controlling the game should have acknowledged the clear evidence of the unacceptable price being paid by players forced too often to replicate the extreme physicality of match play.

Demands for common sense to prevail on this issue were all too rare. In April 2017, a leading expert on brain injuries in sport proved an exception, making a persuasive call for change. Interviewed by BBC Scotland, Dr Willie Stewart, a consultant neuropathologist at Glasgow's Queen Elizabeth University Hospital, suggested a limit on contact training.

"If, during the week, instead of having several days of contact training with more and more impacts on top of each other, you do away with that, you're going to phenomenally reduce the number of impacts over the season and that can't be a bad thing," he said.

"There's a whole lot of unnecessary exposure. Professional rugby players don't forget by Monday or Tuesday how to play rugby, how to tackle, how to go into a ruck. If you want to see the best players playing the best game for as long as possible then it's sensible game management and sensible training management. That's easy and, if World Rugby were serious about it, they would say, 'This is a mandate from on-high, under World Rugby's code, professional players must not do contact training during the season any more than one day a week', for example, or not at all."

For those who questioned his reasoning, Dr Stewart added the damning revelation: "I know some former professional players who looked forward to the weekend match because it gave them a rest. During the week they were just getting destroyed."

The prediction about injuries voiced by John Dawes in

2013 sadly proved all too true. In 2014, England had 10 first-choice players injured. In the 2015 World Cup, Wales, already depleted, lost seven players while Ireland lost their vital quarter-final game versus Argentina without four first-choice players, including their talismanic captain Paul O'Connell and match-winning fly-half Johnny Sexton, injured during a bruising group encounter with France.

Those controlling the game were showing a bewildering lack of sensitivity, failing to realise the burden faced by the modern rugby player. In 2018, World Rugby first voiced their controversial global season plan, proposing to extend the season to 11 months, with increased playing breaks, and the powerfully-built Welsh centre Jamie Roberts labelled it as "crazy".

It was all too clear the many law changes aimed at making the sport more attractive, with the ball longer in play, had failed. For those obsessed with constant motion, there was already a form of rugby union that was almost non-stop action with tries galore. It was called Sevens, it was played in an annual worldwide international series of tournaments and ranked as no more than an entertaining but forgettable diversion from the main game. How many English rugby followers, for example, were aware that in April 2017 in Hong Kong, the electrifying Gloucester-born winger Dan Norton scored his 245th try playing for the England Sevens side, to set a new World Sevens Series record? "Too much champagne," was my late father's telling verdict on this version of rugby.

Dawes's view that it was still possible for 15-a-side teams to play in his London Welsh swift-passing style if the will was there was vividly illustrated on the final day of the 2015 Six Nations tournament. Needing large victories, title contenders put phase rugby on the backburner, resorting to all-out attack. Sensationally, Wales beat Italy 61–20, Ireland defeated Scotland 40–10 and England out-ran France 55–35. For Wales,

George North, for too long starved of decent possession on a diet of "Warrenball" while playing for his country, scored three tries in ten minutes.

The brilliant handling and running skills of the All Blacks side that won the 2015 World Cup later that year also showed defences could be shredded by quick passing and spreading the ball to the flanks without resorting to phase rugby.

Rugby devoted much time to researching concussion and the tiredness levels of players during a game. But no studies revealed whether strength building in the gym had a downside, making players more injury-prone through their muscles and joints losing a degree of elasticity through body building.

But there was a study that offered an insight into the injury problem that resulted in the Rugby Players Association in May 2019 calling for a ban on artificial grass pitches (AGPs). There was a reluctance from some players to play on these surfaces as they lacked the give of a grass surface as well as giving players large, unsightly and painful grazes on their skin. Reality had then backed conjecture when an RFU study revealed that players were averaging 39 days to recover from AGP injuries compared to 30 days for those on grass surfaces, as well as being more prone to lower-limb injuries on synthetic surfaces.

The injury crisis also meant in future years, the UK's NHS is likely to face an unwelcome added cost-burden, catering for the health problems of generations of rugby players paying a price for the sport's physical intensity in the professional era. It was Welsh coach Warren Gatland who speculated on the long-term damage facing the modern rugby player.

"Even I'm scared watching the collisions," he said in November 2017. "We've not seen the impact rugby will have on these young men. What's going to happen to them in the next 10 to 20 years in terms of them needing new knees, new hips, back and neck injuries?"

It was not hard to find evidence backing Gatland's concerns.

"Every morning I get up, walk down the stairs and I struggle," Ugo Monye, the former Harlequins and England wing told a BBC Radio 5 Live podcast in October 2017. "I'm 34. I had a groin reconstruction, I've got tendonitis in both my Achilles. I've got three prolapsed discs in my spine. We've got a new baby at home. I can't actually bend over to pick her up."

Frustratingly, a blueprint to tackle the game's injury crisis did not need to be complex. Merely reversing the law changes and directives that warped the game in the professional era over two decades was the obvious route forward. Why couldn't World Rugby make life easier for referees and simply revert to the traditional law taking tackled players out of the game at the breakdown? Forbidding tackled players handling the ball would have restored a proper contest at the breakdown. The existing "immediate release" law in theory meant players had to place or pass the ball as soon as they were tackled. But their main objective all too often was to see how long they could get away with preventing the opposition getting the ball.

Then ensuring existing laws such as supporting your own bodyweight at the breakdown, binding on a teammate or opponent before joining a ruck or maul were strictly enforced, while penalising players for solo clear-out charges, obstruction and offside offences and bringing back the traditional straight scrum feed, would have transformed the game for the better.

Finally, World Rugby should have returned rugby to its traditional form as a 15-man game rather than a 23-player sport by cutting the substitutes bench to four players, who could only take the field as blood or injury replacements. Banning impact players would hardly have ranked as a radical move. It would simply have taken rugby union back to its heritage, as it wasn't until 1996 that tactical subs were first introduced. With no eight-man subs bench, coaches would no longer have been able to replace half their team and the game would have been safer and fairer.

Former Birmingham and Moseley prop forward Trevor Corless, a member of the Midland Counties (West) side that defeated the All Blacks 16–8 at The Reddings on 6 December 1972, offered an interesting insight into the injustices of players being replaced when we met while both on dog walking duty in Kings Heath Park in south Birmingham in the summer of 2018. Unlike his brother, centre Barrie Corless, he was never capped by his country. But he does have a rueful memory of outplaying his opponent in scrums during an England trial match until his opposite number left the field injured to be replaced by a fresh player. This end result was the equivalent of being faced with an impact player taking the field in the modern game.

"With the present subs rule, it is like getting the better of your opponent in a boxing match for ten rounds then finding him replaced by another fighter," Corless told me.

Former England hooker Brian Moore offered a shrewdly reasoned criticism of the rugby's emergence as a 23-man game in his *Daily Telegraph* column in October 2017, writing: "When you can train players [to play] for limited periods you can accentuate power and size with the attendant injury risks. Add to the fact that some players have to play a full game and are unavoidably tired, you have a physical imbalance that cannot be good.

"Players will no doubt say they cannot be expected to perform at current physical levels for full games but as everyone was in the same position there would be no added injury risk."

Without new players continually taking the field in the latter stages of matches, the game would have been far easier to understand. Undoubtedly there would have been virulent opposition from coaches, clubs and national sides finding their game plans and tactics radically disrupted. But the furore would inevitably have died down in time as the huge benefits of reducing injuries and creating more room for back play as players tired were realised.

The increased size of players and superior fitness levels in the professional era effectively made the 100-metre long rugby field a smaller place. Countering this by extending pitch sizes was unpractical inside the game's major stadiums but there were ways around this seeming impasse. Some suggested the heresy of cutting player numbers to 13, as in rugby league. However, only allowing injury replacements would have effectively increased the size of the field with more gaps appearing as players, notably forwards, inevitably tired in the latter stages of matches. Extending game time from 80 to the 90 minutes a soccer match lasts or stopping the clock after penalty awards were other routes that could have been adopted to create more room as matches drew to a close, by making the players more tired.

It was true, reverting back to an injury-only subs bench would have had considerable downsides. Not only would it have meant a radical rethink of training and coaching techniques but it would also have resulted in coaching and playing redundancies. World Rugby created a generation of players geared to playing rugby as a 23-man sport. Understandably players who were used to playing only part of a match would have resented their roles being radically altered and the possibility of losing their jobs if they failed to meet the different demands of playing an entire 80 minutes. Having spent years gaining coaching qualifications and working out how best to make use of existing laws, coaches at all levels would also have been reluctant to embrace change on such a significant scale, even if it had made their life ultimately easier.

World Rugby could also have argued that the fact the game had become more popular than ever justified retaining the status quo. Aided by brilliant camera coverage, the extreme physicality of modern rugby provided dramatic theatre and often a heightened sense of anticipation for spectators with fresh faces taking the field. There was also something of the gruesome appeal of the gladiatorial brutality of the Roman colosseum games in modern Test rugby, with the shuddering tackles aptly described by commentators as "hits" and brave players displaying the kind of courage you might expect to find in a war zone.

Ireland's epic 16–9 win against New Zealand in Dublin on 17 November 2018, upstaging the game's world champions, was a memorable, bruising and spellbinding encounter. Fittingly, it was a try that would have graced any era of the game that provided the key score, when Irish winger Jacob Stockdale broke the deadlock after taking a pass just beyond the halfway line and outwitting the All Blacks defence with a memorable burst of speed and power, allied to the finesse of gathering his own perfectly weighted kick ahead.

BBC sports writer Tom Fordyce eloquently summed up the faults and virtues of rugby in the professional era in his match report, writing: "Modern rugby is a flawed game. Too much collision, not enough evasion. A season that stretches out and careers too often cut short. Money going where money already is and the hard-up left with even less. And yet, sometimes it produces contests like this, where it drags you in at the start and holds you spellbound for the next 80 minutes, where the brutality has a beauty laced through it, where two sets of players empty themselves of everything they have and even in the last throes, no one is quite sure of who will come out on top."

However, the cost of retaining the status quo in injury terms and a wider public perception of rugby as a dangerous sport became too high, while World Rugby, with characteristic evasiveness, spent years avoiding a dialogue on compelling calls to return rugby as a 15-player sport. World Rugby CEO Brett Gosper and chairman Bill Beaumont never publicly answered the damning question: "How has the eight subs bench laden with impact players turning rugby into a 23-man sport actually benefitted the game?"

The powerful lobby calling for change included: rugby

correspondents Stephen Jones, Nick Cain and Mick Cleary; leading surgeon Professor John Fairclough, a former chairman of the Welsh RFU medical committee; Welsh RFU chairman Gareth Davies, the former Wales fly-half; and famous ex-England internationals Jeremy Guscott, Brian Moore and Jeff Probyn.

*The Sunday Times* rugby correspondent Stephen Jones, in July 2018, produced the most scathing condemnation of allowing tiring players to be replaced, a practice taken from rugby league, writing: "Why on earth did rugby ever pass regulations which allow more than half the starting team to be replaced? Perhaps idiocies are more obvious with hindsight but idiocy it definitely is."

Nick Cain, the chief columnist for *The Rugby Paper*, provided an equally dismissive view of the game's lawmakers in December that year, writing: "The elephant in the room in this injuries debate is the law changes by World Rugby over the last 20 years which has led to the super-sizing of the game.

"Fundamental changes such as allowing eight replacements have altered the aerobic attritional dynamic that is part of the game's tradition completely – and dangerously. It means huge, fresh muscle-bound forwards can be brought on for 20 minutes of powerhouse mayhem."

World Rugby's failure to enforce its own existing rules – those "ghost laws" highlighted by Stephen Jones – was also a major concern. World Rugby argued that if all the laws of the sport were strictly applied top-class rugby would degenerate into matches with endless stoppages in play as players would be constantly penalised. The reality was the reverse was true, as shown when the law forbidding tackles involving the head and neck was finally enforced with a true zero-tolerance policy in the 2019 World Cup in Japan.

Jones also echoed Brendan Gallagher's view on illegal clear-out charges, writing: "You are not meant to crash as individuals into mauls and ruck. You must bind on a colleague before driving in, but this is never applied. What happens these days is that defenceless players who are in rucks and mauls quite legally are smashed off the ball with rhino-like shoulder charges."

Yet, despite all the overwhelming evidence to the contrary, World Rugby's media office still produced the laughable claim those controlling the sport's laws were "committed to achieving clear and consistent decision making."

With the election of the popular former England and Lions captain Bill Beaumont and the great Argentinian scrum-half Agustín Pichot as chairman and vice-chairman of World Rugby in May 2016 came hopes of a new era for the game, with the sport's major problems ranging from the unacceptably high injury count to the huge demands on leading players with the over-congested international calendar, finally being effectively tackled. This duo, plus John Jeffrey, remembered as a member of a wonderful rampaging Scotland back row in a pack that rucked the ball New Zealand style, had been great servants of the game in their playing careers. Occupying key roles with World Rugby, they had the opportunity to do the sport an even greater service, restoring its heritage as a game for all sizes and losing the over-emphasis on power.

But this did not come to pass. Ability on the rugby field and skill as a rugby administrator are rather different qualities.

Just how slowly the wheels moved where World Rugby were concerned was shown by the saga of the three-year residency rule that resulted in major Test nations recruiting Pacific Island players, understandably deserting their poverty-stricken homelands to provide a secure financial future for themselves and their families. From Pichot ("Somebody will kill me but we need to change it") came a commendable but hardly earth-shattering call to extend the residency period from three to five years. But this view was contradicted by World Rugby

CEO Brett Gosper. "There didn't seem any appetite to change it," he maintained. "The World Rugby view is the view of all the unions. There was a consultation with the unions, it was discussed and it was decided it would remain as is."

The fact the major rugby unions were against change was hardly a surprise as there was a significant degree of self-interest, for – with the honourable exception of Argentina and South Africa – they were the countries benefitting from spending years pillaging gifted players from the South Pacific islands.

What was the reasoning behind leaving the law as it was? "The unions didn't have to give reasoning," said Gosper, offering a damning insight into World Rugby's attitude towards accountability that echoed the arrogance of the administrators in the game's past. "They came back and said it is operating in the right way currently at that level of residency."

Was not the integrity of the game under threat? "I think the day when people don't believe they're watching a bona fide international, then you've got problem," said Gosper, turning a Nelsonian blind eye to the issue. "We've got no sign of that."

The fact that the four wingers featuring in the France v Australia game played later that year, in November 2016, were all born in Fiji was hardly indicative there was "no sign" of a problem.

Rugby correspondent Nick Cain summed up the damage done by the existing rule, writing: "World Rugby's three-year residency rule is to blame for turning international rugby into a mercenary free-for-all."

In May 2017, Pichot ("This is a historic moment for the sport") finally had his way when World Rugby adopted a five-year qualifying process. But bafflingly, World Rugby decided to wait until January 2021 to enforce the new residency rule. Beaumont's contorted reasoning for the delay echoed the handiwork of a PR department in full spin mode with the statement: "The extension to the residency period within a forward-thinking reform package will ensure a close, credible and established link between a union and players, which is good for rugby and good for fans."

What was "credible" or "forward-thinking" about leaving the floodgates open until 2021?

Imagining the new ruling would solve the Test mercenaries problem was also somewhat short-sighted. When gifted schoolboy players were being attracted overseas by some nations, a five-year residency rule could hardly be termed effective.

In March 2019, former Wales captain Paul Thorburn, tournament director for the 1999 World Cup, damningly questioned the competence of those controlling the game's destiny for turning the international game into "a laughing stock" having "demonstrated a total lack of vision for the development of the global game". Interviewed by *The Rugby Paper*'s veteran rugby writer Peter Jackson, Thorburn said: "Serious questions need to be raised about their ability to govern the sport. Under the direction of the late Vernon Pugh, World Rugby's predecessor the IRB [International Rugby Board] sent out a mission statement to develop second tier nations like Fiji, Tonga and Samoa.

"He recognised the need for rugby to broaden its base so that we could make the World Cup more competitive and have as many as four countries capable of winning it. Instead it's the same old, same old. Since then, World Rugby have completely undermined that plan by allowing overseas players to qualify through residency for other countries, encouraging the mass influx of players from the South Sea Islands to Europe. They have every right to play wherever they like but they shouldn't be able to switch allegiance from one country to another.

"Until recently you could switch from Fiji to France or Samoa to England or Tonga to Wales in three years, a ridiculously short residential period. Now they have increased it to five but it's nowhere near long enough. If they must have a residential qualification, then make it ten years which is roughly the average length of a professional career.

"It was almost embarrassing to watch Italy play Ireland the other week and see an Irishman [Ian McKinley] representing Italy. There's nothing English about Manu Tuilagi and nothing Welsh about Hadleigh Parkes. What is the justification for that?"

The playing treadmill Test players had to endure provided another example of the damaging reluctance of those controlling rugby's destiny to make decisions for the good of the game lest they upset major rugby nations or clubs, depriving them of revenue. As the great American songwriter/musician Bob Dylan shrewdly observed: "You can't open your mind to every conceivable point of view."

The solution to the vastly overcrowded international fixture calendar was for World Rugby simply to actually place its frequently expressed commitment to player welfare above financial imperatives, by ensuring nations didn't play as many as 11 or 12 Tests a year.

A glance at the career statistics of New Zealand's two greatest forwards illustrated how the demands of Test rugby had changed. In a 15-year international career from 1957–1971, the great New Zealand lock Colin Meads played 55 Tests. By contrast, flanker Richie McCaw in an international career spanning 14 years from 2001–2015 played 148 Tests.

The straightforward answer was to simply end major nations both touring and hosting Tests in the same year, in addition to playing in their annual Six Nations or Rugby Championship tournaments. Why not let a country host a tour one year and go touring the following year? In the past, it was invariably at least a decade before you would find the All Blacks, Springboks or Wallabies repeating a tour of Europe and interest in those tours was huge. By contrast, in 2014 England played five games in the Six Nations in February and March, then toured New Zealand, playing three Tests in June, then played New Zealand, South Africa, Samoa and Australia in the November autumn internationals at Twickenham.

Did playing the All Blacks four times in a year make sense? Why couldn't World Rugby, controlling international fixtures, have simply changed the system so if England had a summer tour of New Zealand, their players would avoid the huge physical demands of also playing November internationals just a few months later. Then, the following year, New Zealand would not host a Test series, but would tour Europe, while England would have a free summer and play autumn internationals against a touring side.

Reducing the Test match schedule from 12 to nine fixtures a year, as well as giving players a genuine escape from the Test treadmill and abandoning autumn internationals would have enabled the hugely popular traditional rugby tours to be revived, in a shortened form. The All Blacks, Australia, South Africa or Argentina could have embarked on a seven- or eight-match tour, playing Tests against a home nation as well as games against leading club and provincial sides.

Saracens won both the Premiership and the European Champions Cup in the 2018–19 season and people were speculating about whether they were better than national sides. Revive the traditional rugby tour and the answer could have been provided. Imagine the appeal of the All Blacks playing Saracens (before the salary cap scandal engulfed the club) at Twickenham on an England tour. Similarly, there would have been huge interest in say Leinster playing South Africa in Dublin, the Scarlets facing the New Zealanders, trying to repeat Llanelli's fabled 1972 win against the men in black, or Glasgow taking on the Australians.

Reviving rugby tours was common sense. You were hardly venturing into unknown territory. The only surviving traditional rugby tour undertaken every four years – the British & Irish

113

Lions tour – was more popular than ever, as well as a huge financial success.

Tours could have involved as few as six, seven or eight games, as the All Blacks or England, for example, would not have been scratch sides like the Lions, who needed time playing together to be at their most effective. Tours would also have reaffirmed the reality that Test rugby and matches involving national sides playing clubs and provinces has always been the lifeblood of the sport and its most profitable avenue.

England's leading rugby clubs might have cast an envious eye at the riches available to their soccer equivalents. But as well as rugby union being far too complex and physical a sport to match soccer's appeal, there would have been a downside to the oval ball club scene attempting to match the appeal of Test rugby, with money deciding the strength of clubs.

On 17 April 2019, Tottenham Hotspur sensationally knocked Manchester City out of the Champions League on the away goal rule, despite their 4–3 second leg defeat, watched by 53,348 spectators at the Etihad Stadium in Manchester. In a compelling match hailed as a classic encounter between two leading English soccer clubs, there were just five Englishmen among the 22 players in the starting line-up for both sides. Did rugby really want to go down that path, eroding its integrity? Older rugby followers will remember the sense of excitement and anticipation when the All Blacks and Springboks toured Britain in the amateur era, years, sometimes even decades, after they had previously been seen north of the equator. And how anticipation grew in the build-up to Tests as leading clubs, provinces and combined sides tried, generally in vain, to beat the tourists.

How many other sports have books written about a single match? Llanelli's famous 9–3 victory against the 1972–73 All Blacks is remembered in Alun Gibbard's book *Who Beat the All Blacks?* and Max Boyce's tribute ballad '9–3', while Alan English's book *Stand Up and Fight – When Munster beat the All*

*Blacks* narrates the Irish province's immortalised 12–0 victory against the 1978 All Blacks.

Rugby tour matches have never been treated as "friendlies". Covering the 1935–36 All Blacks tour of Britain for the *New Zealand Herald*, my late father Wallace Reyburn witnessed the Welsh club Swansea, with the schoolboy half-backs Haydn Tanner and Willie Davies, defeat the tourists 11–3. Four decades later, having remained north of the equator, writing his book *The Winter Men* on the Seventh All Blacks tour, he watched Llanelli – inspired by their coach Carwyn James – defeat the tourists. Describing a fixture that saw a small south Wales town's rugby side take on the world's greatest rugby nation, he found the game matched the intensity of a Test match. He wrote: "There is a look that comes over the faces of the touring All Blacks in the course of a match when it becomes clear they are going to be beaten. It's not just disappointment. It's a look of shame that they have let their country down.

"I remember most vividly seeing it at Swansea in 1935 because that was the first time I saw it. After a run of 36 All Black victories in Britain on the trot, here was this new side going down 11–3 to Swansea ... And again there was that same look on the faces of these Seventh All Blacks as Andy Hill put over a 50-yard penalty to take Llanelli into the final minutes with a lead there seemed no chance of wresting from a team playing like demons, urged on by a crowd so fervid that for these young new tourists Stradey Park reeked of animosity."

Unions may have regarded the loss of any Test revenue with some dread but the long-term benefits to both players and the sport's popularity of a less crowded Test calendar and the revival of the traditional rugby tour in a shortened form should not have been ignored. What was more important – financial imperatives or reducing the heavy injury toll inflicted on leading players?

If paying more than lip service to player welfare meant players receiving less money and more realistic financial budgeting, then so be it. The loss of Test revenue wouldn't have been as damaging as imagined. Making Test rugby a more exclusive event and reviving the traditional tour would undoubtedly have heightened interest in the sport for both players and spectators, adding to sponsorship appeal.

However, for World Rugby to make a decisive decision against the wishes of the major unions, who were unwilling to sacrifice any Test revenue, was a step too far.

The intense competitiveness of the English Premiership, with the 12 clubs playing a minimum of 22 games spread over nine months and leading clubs also facing a formidable European Champions Cup programme, placed a huge burden on English Test players, who were expected to turn out for their clubs regularly when not playing for their country. The 2018 Six Nations offered evidence that the vast demands had taken their toll in terms of exhaustion, as the England side, coached by Eddie Jones, that had won 18 consecutive fixtures and two consecutive Six Nations, finished fifth that year, losing their three final matches – a loss total that was to stretch to five in a row when England toured South Africa that summer.

However instead of cutting Test fixtures, World Rugby, seduced by the prospect of the Swiss sports marketing firm Infront providing £6.1 billion over 12 years in a partnership offer, produced a misguided masterplan for a global Test championship spread over 11 months. Fronted by the then World Rugby vice-chairman Pichot, the proposal involved creating an annual 12-country Nations Championship to decide the leading rugby country outside World Cup years.

All hell broke loose in March 2019 after the *New Zealand Herald* newspaper detailed the plan could involve replacing the annual June and November tours with a tournament involving the Six Nations teams meeting their Rugby Championship rivals with the United States and Japan thrown into the 12-country mix at the expense of the Pacific Island countries, who would be relegated to a second-tier championship. Such was the backlash against the concept that Fiji, Samoa and Tonga, whose formidable production line of gifted rugby players enhances the worldwide game, threatened to boycott the 2019 World Cup.

"Now is the time for the voice of Pacific rugby to be heard through our players," said Daniel Leo, the former Samoan lock, arguing it was "abundantly clear that World Rugby has failed the genuine rugby fan".

*Daily Telegraph* rugby reporter Ben Coles agreed, writing: "World League plans are a disgrace. Everything about the new proposed World League reeks of greed and leaves a bad taste in the mouth."

Leading world players also joined the tidal wave of criticism. "To suggest that players can play five incredibly high-level Test matches in consecutive weeks in November shows little understanding of the physical strain this brings," said Ireland's Johnny Sexton. The much respected All Blacks captain Kieran Read also condemned the initiative, stating: "Fans want to see meaningful games; they don't want to see fatigued players playing a reduced quality of rugby as part of a money-driven, weakened competition that doesn't work for the players and clubs."

World Rugby did its best to quell the outcry, pointing out no format had been finalised. But whatever form the Nations Championship took it would effectively be a competition to find the best Test side in the world that would diminish the value of the World Cup while doing nothing to ease the unacceptable playing burden on Test players. Had not the rugby tour been an effective yardstick for judging the world's best rugby country?

It was easy to see why World Rugby, treating finance as a priority, sought to get the USA and Japan, two of the world's major economic powers, into the rugby front line. But a degree of realism was needed. Attempts to convert Americans to rugby union had had little significant impact in denting the vast popularity of their main oval ball sport, American football. While

Japan's enthusiasm for rugby was unquestionable, the fact is, they are a relatively small nation in stature terms, making it highly unlikely they would ever compete effectively enough to win the World Cup – unless World Rugby significantly reduced the sport's physicality.

Such was the backlash against the flawed scheme, World Rugby chairman Beaumont entered peacemaker mode, declaring "Contrary to reports, no decisions have been made." His statement succeeded in lowering the flimsy credibility of the concept even further through his media department clumsily referring to "ongoing speculation and inaccurate information in the public sphere, which World Rugby cannot yet publicly address owing to the fluid and sensitive nature".

It is difficult to believe his team talks as the England and Lions captain in his playing days could have matched this level of PR gobbledegook.

The problem facing Test rugby was not the product but the fact rugby administrators were unable to realise the damage being done to the sport by the hugely over-congested fixtures schedule at both club and Test level. However, it was unrealistic to pretend fewer Test matches alone could have solved the game's injury crisis.

Nor did anybody believe you could make rugby a safe sport. As Professor Fairclough, a leading expert on rugby injuries, shrewdly pointed out: "Some sports recognise they have inherent harm, sport being a major source of injuries. *Volenti non fit injuria* is the legal term where it is accepted that an individual will anticipate being hurt but accepts that is part of sport. Rugby in its nature is a sport where contact has not only been part of the game but relished."

In the winter of 2018–2019, the RFU sought to reduce injuries by reducing the tackle below shoulder level in the Championship Cup but abandoned the experiment after concussions increased as players bent at the waist carrying the ball. However much you lower tackles, you can never guarantee safety, as I am only too well aware, having been involved as a young journalist with English rugby's most high-profile serious casualty when I was acting as the ghost-writer for former England international Danny Hearn's autobiography *Crash Tackle*, published in 1972. Playing for the Home Counties and the Midlands against the 1967 All Blacks at Leicester, Hearn, renowned as a tackler, broke his neck trying to bring down his strongly built opposite number Ian MacRae with a traditional tackle. His injury was the result of misjudging his tackle as his head thudded into his opponent's hip rather than behind the second five-eighth's body. The book detailed Hearn's long, courageous battle against full paralysis below the neck.

Rugby's problem in the modern era was not the tackle *per se* but the sheer volume of tackles and resulting breakdown illegalities. Abandoning unsuccessful law changes that had caused the injury crisis would hardly have been a major return to rugby's amateur era, when the game had many faults.

Footage of the legendary 1971 Lions team drawing their fourth Test against New Zealand in Auckland 14–14 vividly illustrated rugby's downsides before it went professional. On a showery afternoon, the lineouts were a chaotic lottery in an error-ridden game while scrums were frequently in constant motion before the ball was fed. Unhappy at being obstructed in the lineout, schoolmaster Graham Whiting floored Gordon Brown with a haymaker punch in front of the referee, who merely awarded a penalty to the Lions. All Blacks prop Brian 'Jazz' Muller escaped censure for blatant use of the boot and JPR Williams left Muller a dazed wreck, hurling him into touch with a thunderous shoulder charge tackle.

These examples of dangerous play became unheard of with the advent of sophisticated television coverage and punitive penalties. As Ellis Genge, the highly rated, fiery young Leicester and England prop forward, remarked in October 2017 when asked about on the field violence: "Aggro? I've had worse down the off-licence."

Wingers in that Auckland Test threw in lineout ball and the Lions surrendered six points through penalties for a Gareth Edwards crooked scrum feed and flanker Peter Dixon straying offside by a foot or so without affecting play. Neither of these offences would have been penalised in recent years, with World Rugby intent on keeping the game flowing. The video shows players respecting referee John Pring's decisions. Scrums were sorted out by the opposing packs in seconds with no collapsing, with referee intervention only occurring when they needed to be straightened or scrum-halves gave away a penalty for a crooked feed.

Oddly, the attacking skills of that great Lions backline, which had destroyed leading New Zealand provincial sides, were hardly in evidence during the game, as the tourists resorted to safety-first kicking, seeking a series win rather than tries with their ample possession opportunities in the game's final quarter.

Ironically, rugby's amateur era was more violent, with forwards regularly punching each other, but in the professional age, with the endless physical confrontation, it became more dangerous, with backs as well as forwards involved in high injury rates. However forward power was always a major feature of the sport and an integral part of its appeal. One of the most awesome sights produced by the sport was provided by the great All Blacks pack dominating Test rugby during the 1960s with their rampaging runs and wonderfully coordinated rucking skills, delivering the ball back to their scrum-half in the distant days when tackled players generally avoided illegally blocking the ball for reasons of self- preservation.

Despite its over-emphasis on power, modern rugby had much to commend it. The brilliantly sophisticated television coverage made top-grade rugby compelling theatre and put an end to the naked violence of the past. With a video referee officially called a TMO (television match official) as well as touch judges (or referee's assistants) helping the main referee, penalty offences became that much easier to detect, adding a sense of drama to match viewing. The 10-minute sin bin, universally introduced in 2000, proved an inspired piece of legislation, allowing referees to effectively punish lawbreakers without resorting to the draconian red card.

Unlike the past, the modern lineouts were a highly skilled, clear-cut source of quick clean ball, and most impressive of all was the standard of defence. When Wales beat Ireland 23–16 at the Millennium Stadium in Cardiff on 14 March 2015, they survived 32 phases as the Irish unsuccessfully tried to batter their way over the Welsh try line from just feet away. The success of the 2017 Lions in drawing an epic three-Test series in New Zealand owed much to their wonderful defence, masterminded by the coaching of former rugby league star Andy Farrell.

World Rugby could have transformed the modern game by combining the best of the past with the present. Returning the straight feed to the commendable modern but theatrically slow-paced "crouch, bind, set" instruction that lessened the impact of the far bigger modern packs merging at scrum time could have created the ideal set piece: a steady scrum, the return of the art of hooking the ball and ball provided for the backs in space. Yet, despite the hugely detailed television coverage and the TMO, players continued to be allowed to get away with a whole raft of offences in the so-called interests of keeping the game flowing.

When 2017 drew to a close, following the huge interest created by the Lions drawing their series with the world champions and aided by the success of the Sevens tournament in the 2016 Olympic Games in Brazil, numbers playing the game worldwide had risen to 8.5 million, more than double the 2009 figure, with a large increase in women playing the sport. Opening World Rugby's 13th general assembly in London on 13 November 2017, chairman Bill Beaumont told delegates: "At the heart of everything we do will be our values of integrity, solidarity, discipline, respect and passion and I will ensure that this continues to be central to our decision-making process."

However, this lofty assertion was severely dented two days later when the secret ballot involving 31 council members resulted in France being chosen as hosts of the 2023 World Cup. There is little doubt France, as a great rugby nation, will stage a successful event. But the decision flew in the face of the clear recommendation from the Rugby World Cup Limited Board a fortnight earlier backing the specially commissioned 139-page report that came out strongly in favour of South Africa hosting the tournament ahead of France and third-placed Ireland. Instead of backing the report it had commissioned, the Board decided to leave the final vote to the council members with their differing agendas of self-interest. The fact France, with its huge financial potential, won the final vote showed a worrying degree of weak leadership and a characteristic inability to make decisions for the good of the game, without consultation.

Neither does a detailed examination of the moral high ground with its emphasis on integrity and respect described by Beaumont match what happened since the game of rugby union turned professional. Ensuring top level referees ignored one of the game's key laws – the straight scrum feed – for more than a decade and refusing to enter a public debate on the issue had little to do with integrity.

Player welfare could hardly be termed a main priority when charging full pelt illegally into opponents who hadn't even got the ball at the breakdown was continually tolerated. As Sir Colin Meads, who was hardly a saint on the rugby field, said before he died in 2017: "This isn't sport, it is an assault that should have no place on a rugby field."

Those who regarded this view as an exaggeration should have heeded the words of leading rugby agent Shaun Longstaff, the former Scotland wing. Back in August 2016 he offered BBC Scotland journalist Jamie Lyall a hugely disturbing insight into the priority given to physicality. He pointed out some elite club coaches had players wearing sensors measuring G-force when players tackled, collided or hit a ruck and added: "It's definitely a game of how big can we get players. The main theme is violence at the breakdown for certain directors of rugby. There are coaches who openly talk about the G-force on the hits ... I don't know the way forward, I just know that I'm worried, and have been for ages."

To its credit, the IRB/World Rugby oversaw a huge growth in the professional era, no doubt due to the marketing skills of Brett Gosper, who was appointed CEO of the IRB in 2012. The World Rugby Hall of Fame, opened in 2016 in the Warwickshire town of Rugby, provided an impressively curated exhibition, making inventive use of modern technology offering a fascinating insight into the game's past. But the fact remained, the game's unacceptably high injury statistics were a sad indictment of the way IRB/World Rugby ran the sport during the first two decades of the professional era.

The fact World Rugby's leaders were in denial an injury crisis even existed hardly helped matters. Gosper's claim, made in 2016, that the sport was "safer than ever" had a distinctly hollow ring when no less than 41 Test players were sidelined, unfit to play for their countries in the autumn internationals played in November 2017.

In December 2017, British rugby correspondent Stephen Jones in *The Sunday Times* provided a stark condemnation of the reality facing the sport, writing: "The sport puts commercial needs above the murderous toll it takes on players. Is there anyone out there grasping the reality of modern rugby and phase after phase of giants banging heads who does not believe this kind of itinerary is beyond crazy and approaching a criminal offence ... And still nobody takes a black pen to the fixture list."

Yet that same month you found World Rugby chairman

Beaumont voicing the complacent assertion: "We must ensure that rugby continues to be a leader in sport in the prevention and management of injury."

Four months later, in April 2018, there was disturbing evidence increasing numbers of players were finding their rugby careers ending because of the dangers in the sport. That month Dragons centre Adam Hughes retired from rugby after receiving medical advice. He was the third member of the same Welsh club in three seasons to retire from the game after head injuries. At the end of the month, on 29 April, former England winger-turned-broadcaster Ugo Monye on a Radio 5 Live Sport podcast paid tribute to the modern rugby player saying: "These guys are modern-day gladiators. They give absolutely everything every weekend. They go out there for our entertainment and sometimes it costs people their careers and the way they function for the rest of their lives."

Then, in July 2018 came a telling high-profile insight into what the modern rugby player has to endure, when the universally admired Wales and Lions captain Sam Warburton, at the relatively young age of 29, retired from rugby, deciding he could no longer meet the intense physical demands of the modern game.

"My body is unable to give me back what I had hoped for on my return," he told the media. His sorry medical CV included no less than 20 significant injuries sidelining him during his 11 years on the game's frontline. The damage toll included two dislocations, a fractured cheekbone, a broken jaw, concussion and knee surgery.

Warburton's retirement reignited the calls for ending impact subs to make the sport less dangerous. Professor John Fairclough once again called for reform, stating: "The game I saw in the 1970s and 1980s is not the game I see now and I think that substitutions should be for injury, not for impact. The difficulty is there are a lot of vested interests. My vested interest is in trying to keep people healthy and I do think we have to look at the consequences, not just now – Sam's got to live the consequences the rest of his life from 29 onwards."

Another factor heightening the need for reform making the game safer was the prospect of legal claims by players seriously injured playing rugby union. In 2018, Sale scrum-half Cillian Willis decided to take legal action against his club and two doctors after he retired after suffering concussion playing against Saracens in 2013. He alleged he was allowed to play on and then suffered a second blow to the head.

Leading injury claims lawyer Steven Baylis, a partner with Lime Personal Injury, warned that rugby could face more claims in the future, telling *The Observer* newspaper:

"Injuries do seem to be on the increase. Clubs will have to be put on alert by what is happening in America. Issues that need to be looked at include whether overtraining causes weaknesses or too much lifting heavy weights can predispose players to injury. With the intensity top players operate at, I think the season is too long."

But those controlling the game saw no need for major change. Addressing the World Rugby Medical Commission Conference held in London on 1–2 November, 2018, Beaumont was again firmly in denial mode and told delegates: "As a father of rugby-playing sons, a fan and chairman of World Rugby, I am committed to ensuring that our sport leads the way in injury prevention, management and education.

"Through collaboration with our unions and independent medical experts, we are constantly conducting evidence-based research ... Together, we have worked hard to implement evidence-based programmes that standardise best practice in injury-management, and the research strongly indicates that great strides have been made."

A major problem facing the sport was professional rugby players were understandably unwilling to risk damaging their career prospects by criticising the way the game was being run. Few would dispute Brian Moore's view that meaningful change making rugby safer was "not easy". But the worryingly defeatist view Damian Hopley, chief executive of the Rugby Players Association, expressed in October 2018 was less credible. He stated: "Injuries are an occupational hazard and at this point it is hard to say how we can reduce them."

Did Hopley really believe returning rugby as a 15-man sport and reducing the fixtures treadmill would not cut injury levels? Would not ending players charging full pelt into players in illegal solo clear-out charges really not make the game a little safer?

In December 2018, Beaumont's optimistic assessment of the sport looked woefully out of tune with reality with the death of 19-year-old Nicolas Chauvin after his neck had been broken in a double tackle playing in a youth match. The Stade Français player was the third French youngster to die as a result of playing rugby in just eight months. Weeks later, in January 2019, the tragic French death count rose to four when Nathan Soyeux, a 23-year-old university student who had been injured while being tackled during a match in November, died in hospital.

"Rugby kills because with professionalisation a rough game has become a violent game," was the alarming verdict of the sports magazine *L'Équipe* after Chauvin's death.

World Rugby's Gosper and Beaumont crossed the Channel to meet French Rugby Federation president Bernard Laporte, who called for a fundamental change, returning rugby to "a game of movement where avoidance overrides the impact".

But the French, with various tackle-law suggestions, and Beaumont promising "We will exhaust all recourse in our unwavering commitment to continue our efforts to reduce injury" seemed lost for effective answers for the crisis. World Rugby's commitment to exploring all avenues had a distinctly hollow ring as it had showed no evidence of paying any heed to years of calls from ex-internationals and rugby writers for the return of rugby as a 15-man sport. Mankind has landed men on the moon. Was it really beyond human ingenuity to make a highly physical sport played in the controlled environment of a sports field 100 metres long safer?

In December 2018, Bill Beaumont was given a knighthood in the Queen's New Year's Honours List for his services to rugby. Earlier that month his claim "great strides" had been made under his guidance was contradicted when *Rugby World* magazine provided a telling insight into the unhappy realities of modern rugby with its player survey involving 350 Test players. The fact 74% of the players admitted they had been concussed was far from the only worrying statistic produced by the survey.

Before the 2019 World Cup started in Japan in September, World Rugby announced its series of "ground breaking" law amendments to be trialled in 2020. Once more, flawed solutions tinkering with existing laws was the order of the day. The 50/22 law suggestion to be trialled in Australia was an unwelcome contradiction of one of the fundamental laws of rugby union – i.e. you kick to touch in open play and the opposition have a throw-in. The ruling meant a kick from your own half going indirectly into touch in the opposition 22 would earn you a lineout throw-in. The rationale behind this was to create space by forcing players to drop back out of the defensive line in order to prevent their opponents kicking to find touch. But this move, like the crooked put-in, was warping a distinctive element of the union game. Was it that hard to visualise a kicker in the great Welsh fly-half Barry John's class having a field day, earning lineouts for his team in the opposition's 22 using this rule?

The one obvious major change – the end of impact subs – that could have transformed the game was considered by World Rugby's executive committee. But with typical indecisiveness, it avoided trialling this all too obvious route to making rugby a safer sport. Instead it was decided World

Rugby would "sponsor more research to determine if there is a player welfare benefit". Had not two decades of impact subs hitting the field termed "an idiocy" by *Sunday Times* rugby correspondent Stephen Jones provided enough evidence?

The great irony was, while rugby union became ever more popular in the professional era as a spectator sport, the numbers of male players taking up the game in major rugby-playing countries such as England and Wales were dwindling. While leading players had the compensation of fame and being financially well rewarded for what was, for many, an injury-ridden existence, it was a different scenario in the game's schools and amateur ranks where many felt the game was too physical to accept the *volenti non fit injuria* principle, acknowledging injuries as part of the sport.

Little may have seemed wrong with New Zealand rugby, with the All Blacks dominating the world scene, with their successive World Cup wins in 2011 and 2015 rewarding the population's devotion to rugby. But sports writer Gregor Paul, writing in the *New Zealand Herald* in February 2019, produced an apocalyptic view of rugby's future as a popular grassroots sport. He wrote: "Just as it turned out that the *Titanic* wasn't too big to sink, New Zealand rugby is not too big to fail. It may be preposterous to see a dystopian future when New Zealand Rugby banked a record profit last year from record revenue driven by the continued excellence of its national teams. But there is a massive hole in the hull and just like the *Titanic*, the game here is in danger of sinking.

"The collapse has become a distinct possibility following NZR's commissioned review into schools rugby which has revealed just how steeply playing numbers are falling among teenage boys. Rugby is categorically not the game of choice for boys aged 13–18. Figures from the last three years show that around 3,000 boys give up rugby between the ages of 10 and 13. Of those who were still playing at 13, more than half were lost to rugby by the time they were 18.

"If the trend continues, rugby will cease to exist as a grassroots sport. Instead of being the national game, entwined in the social fabric of the country, it will be, for males at least, played only by the elite. The concept of playing rugby for fun will be dead. Gone from the Saturday morning landscape will be humans of all shapes, sizes and abilities chasing a ball around a muddy field, not because they see a future career in it, but because, as ridiculous as it may be, they genuinely love doing it.

"And it is even harder to believe that a world league of rugby or whatever nonsense is being conjured up in Los Angeles is going to do anything other than accelerate rugby's transition in New Zealand from being a mass participation sport to a mass spectator sport."

Similarly, Professor Fairclough, early in 2019, had provided me with a worrying picture of youth rugby in Wales suffering decreasing numbers. Not long afterwards in Birmingham, I met a former club cricket colleague who still kept active refereeing junior rugby matches in the West Midlands. And he sadly narrated the difficulties clubs at grassroots level were experiencing fielding several teams due to declining player numbers. The junior club I played for ran five Saturday sides in the early 1980s but now was down to two sides.

Visiting a coffee bar in Shakespeare's birthplace town, Stratford-upon-Avon, in Warwickshire in December 2018, I had been offered a sad insight into the all too real crisis facing rugby. At a table next to me, a couple debated what rugby kit to buy their young son for Christmas. He had a great time playing mini rugby with 25 other kids at a Cotswold rugby club's Sunday morning sessions. But the mother added quite firmly they would stop him playing the game when tackling replaced touch rugby.

It was some 35 years since Carwyn James sadly died in an Amsterdam hotel room aged just 53 and John Dawes's direct involvement in the game had long since passed. But if the common sense solutions they advocated that would have ended the modern game's injury crisis had been adopted, rugby union's debt to these two visionaries from the Welsh Valleys need not have ended.

## Blueprint for Change

Ten measures that would have transformed rugby in the first 25 years of the game's professional era.

1)  Ending tackled players handling the ball.

2)  Restoring the traditional straight scrum feed.

3)  Lowering tackle height to below shoulder level.

4)  Restoring rugby union as a 15-player sport by reducing the substitutes bench from eight to four players, who could only take the field as blood or injury replacements.

5)  Ending the Test match treadmill by restricting nations to nine rather than 12 internationals a year.

6)  A ten-year residency rule to end players switching countries with no family links.

7)  Transforming the finances of the Pacific Island rugby nations by giving Fiji, Samoa and Tonga reasonable gate money for playing Tests in Europe.

8)  Strictly enforcing existing rules ending solo clear outs, offsides, obstructing opponents and other laws going unpunished.

9)  Ending referees warning players not to commit offences.

10) Making use of yellow cards to ensure only a side's captain could speak to a referee to query decisions during a match.

CHAPTER 7

# Has Rugby Union Lost its Values?

*Telling a referee "It's clear as day, mate!" is hardly
a great advert for the game's manners.*

THE ETHOS OF rugby union's amateur era, when players rarely questioned a referee's decision, ended after the sport turned professional. Two decades later, far too frequently you found captains politely asking for decisions to be clarified or pointing out missed examples of law breaking. Addressing a referee respectfully as "Sir" hardly masked the fact in the hands of any decent lawyer this would rank as dissent. Professional players should not have needed to have the laws of the sport they play explained during play.

In a sport where distance matters, referees had a straightforward solution to ending their decisions being queried by players. As Nick Cain, chief writer for *The Rugby Paper*, wrote in January 2017: "Constant appealing of decisions to referees and assistant referees should incur a penalty, with a ten-metre march-back, and then a yellow card. The ten-metre march for dissent is a great deterrent, and one that referees do not utilise enough – especially at a time when there is more chat on the pitch than on *The Graham Norton Show*."

Occasionally, but not often enough, referees used their powers to put a stop to the undermining of their authority by players. When Exeter ended Saracens' 22-match unbeaten record with a 31–13 victory at Sandy Park in Devon on 22

131

December 2018, referee Thomas Foley gave the home side a penalty after tiring of Owen Farrell constantly debating his decisions. Earlier in the year, on 20 January, Wayne Barnes threatened to go a step further when the formidable former All Black centre Ma'a Nonu playing for Toulon told him: "That's a yellow!" demanding a Scarlets player be sent to the sin bin during a heated European Champions Cup encounter in Llanelli that ended in an unexpected 30–27 win for the Welsh side. "Let's make it really clear," Barnes told Nonu. "You come and ask for a yellow card, you get one. Understand?" Few would have criticised Barnes if he had simply given the former All Black a yellow card rather than a warning.

Elite rugby referees generally deserved high marks for the impressive way they handled the most complex of sports with players all too often playing on the edge of legality. Officiating with microphones so every word they said could be heard beyond the field of play, they also went well beyond the call of duty, constantly warning players not to commit offences such as illegally playing the ball or going offside. Quite why they felt obliged to help players who were professionals, and who should have been fully aware of the rules of the sport they played, made little sense to neutral observers. Strictly penalising players for lawbreaking was the way to ensure rules were obeyed, but the World Rugby obsession with keeping the game flowing held sway.

The fact the TMO could give a verdict on foul play and debatable tries saw the authority of referees undermined further by players as they too frequently requested video replays, hoping to get rulings in their side's favour.

It was totally unreasonable to expect officials to get every decision right. But for some players, coaches, commentators and spectators it was too much to accept the game's traditional stance that the referee was always right even when he was wrong, while players constantly made mistakes. By contrast, in rugby league players just obeyed rulings by the referee without any questioning or dissent.

The one black mark on an otherwise hugely successful 2015 World Cup was the vilification of South African referee Craig Joubert, blamed for depriving Scotland of a sensational quarter-final win against Australia at Twickenham. His crime was awarding Australia what proved a match-winning penalty, ruling Scottish forward Jon Welsh had made the schoolboy error of handling the ball in what seemed an obvious offside position, as he was ahead of play. Joubert, and incidentally also his two touch judges, had failed to realise Welsh was in fact onside as Australian scrum-half Nick Phipps had previously made contact with the ball in a scramble for possession just after a Scottish player knocked it on, a moment not easy to detect without the benefit of slow-motion replays.

At the end of the game, Joubert sprinted towards the tunnel instead of staying on the pitch to shake hands with the players. Television viewers were then subjected to hearing an apoplectic former Scotland captain Gavin Hastings demanding Joubert "should be sent home now" while fellow commentator, former England scrum-half Matt Dawson, was equally embarrassing, acting as judge and jury ranting: "Craig Joubert, you are a disgrace and should never referee again! How dare you sprint off the pitch after that decision!"

The reality was, with the destiny of the game in their hands, Scotland not Joubert lost the match through two successive blunders – a misdirected lineout throw followed by that knock-on, with just two minutes play left. Rugby's rules didn't permit Joubert to go to the TMO to review his ruling. Even if Joubert had made the right decision, a Scotland victory was no certainty for there would have been a scrum in Australia's favour for the knock-on. Certainly, the fact Joubert ran off the field after blowing the final whistle, avoiding a hostile atmosphere, hardly helped his cause. But far more disturbing than anything that had happened during the match was the fact in a sport renowned for its post-match camaraderie a referee felt the need to depart the field so abruptly.

France, in fact, had far more cause to be upset by Joubert's refereeing. In the 2011 World Cup final in Auckland, New Zealand, displaying a palpable degree of stage fright, won the match by a narrow 8–7 margin after Joubert had allowed the All Blacks to get away with a succession of blatant penalty offences at the breakdown as the game reached a climax, depriving the unpredictable French, who had stuttered their way to the final after losing to Tonga in a group match, of victory.

Although rugby came nowhere near to matching the way soccer players berate officials, disturbingly respect for the referees had sadly been eroded. On 29 May 2016 in the England–Wales encounter at Twickenham there was the embarrassing spectacle of the impressively competitive but petulant Welsh fly-half Dan Biggar staging an unseemly soccer-style rant at the Italian referee Marius Mitrea for awarding England back row forward Jack Clifford a try. Biggar continually claimed it should have been disallowed for a previous knock-on offence that even video replays failed to detect. A firmer referee would have told Biggar to accept the decision or leave the field.

The Biggar episode was no isolated example of rugby players reprimanding referees. In England's 30–6 win against Australia at Twickenham on 18 November 2017, the young New Zealand referee Ben O'Keeffe had to endure two players railing at him. Owen Farrell, captaining England after Dylan Hartley had been substituted, in the words of rugby columnist Stuart Barnes "bullied" the 28-year-old referee into checking an offside obstruction offence before Australia crossed the try line. Farrell telling a referee, "It's clear as day, mate!" was hardly a great advert for the game's manners. Later, Australian full-back Kurtley Beale, with unseemly vehemence, persistently disputed being sent to the sin bin after blocking a pass with an outstretched arm that prevented a potential England try.

Sadly, trends at the game's highest level were inevitably

translated down to grassroots and schools level. In March 2016, a *Daily Telegraph* investigation surveying more than 100 referees found 67% had been subjected to abuse. Of those, 90% reported that it was verbal while, more disturbingly, 10% said that it was physical. And the evidence was the situation was getting worse. A clear majority – 74% – said that it was increasing and affecting their enjoyment of the game, while an overwhelming majority – 96% – agreed there had been an erosion of respect and sportsmanship against the values of rugby.

In March 2017, the National Schools Rugby Tournament, with RFU approval, introduced new rules as there had been "a downward drift" in touchline behaviour in the junior game generally. The penalties ranged up to a maximum six points deduction for sides whose touchline supporters were guilty of "poor sportsmanship, a clear and repetitive lack of respect for the referee and his decisions". A far more effective remedy would have been a true zero-tolerance approach, with referees telling touchline offenders they would have to leave the game if the abuse continued, and if they refused to go, simply abandoning the match and awarding victory to the side with the better-behaved support.

It was really up to clubs to preserve the game's manners. Speaking to a lifelong servant of Birmingham's Moseley rugby club, I asked how they dealt with abusive spectators at youth matches. "They are told they are not wanted at the club," was the straightforward reply.

Another worrying feature was the increasing lack of respect some players showed for their opponents. The sight of players in gloat mode, congratulating opponents or condescendingly patting them on the head when they gave away penalties, was not an example you would want followed at grassroots or schools level. It may have been unrealistic to expect the return of the Corinthian sporting ethic in the professional era. But if clubs were not prepared to ensure their players behaved in a reasonable way, referees should have applied the law which states "A player must not do anything against the spirit of good sportsmanship in the playing enclosure" and penalised players for things like mocking opponents, trying to get them to give penalties and feigning injury, which, thankfully, was only an occasional sight.

Despite these unhappy trends, rugby ensured players at elite level who abused referees were heavily punished, in sharp contrast to what happened on the soccer field. The penalties imposed on Premier League soccer players remained laughable. On 25 April 2016, Leicester forward Jamie Vardy was given a mere extra one-match ban for referee abuse to add to his existing one-game ban for his red card during his side's 2–2 draw with West Ham on 17 April. Astonishingly, England football manager Roy Hodgson said Vardy's reaction to Jon Moss's decision was understandable as it was debatable he deserved a red card. "He is a human being and that can happen," he said of the forward's angry outburst. Did the amiable Hodgson really feel an England player calling the referee "a f****** c***" was acceptable?

Rugby could not claim to be free of referee abuse but at least the sport had a zero-tolerance policy when players hit red mist levels. Contrasting with the one-match ban handed to Vardy, future England captain Dylan Hartley was sent off for calling referee Wayne Barnes "a f****** cheat" while playing for Northampton against Leicester in May 2013 and was given an 11-week ban, despite his claim the abuse was directed at an opposition player. The judgment cost him a career highlight in the form of a place on the 2013 British & Irish Lions tour of Australia.

Happily, rugby still did not suffer from crowd trouble. An old Saracens friend recalled an interesting experience when he was with a few hundred England supporters drinking heavily in a bar in a Rome square before an England match against Italy. Facing the supporters was a line of police assembled to prevent trouble. After a while my friend approached the inspector heading the operation telling him: "We're not football supporters, there won't be any trouble." Back came the reply: "I know that. You know that. But we're on double time!"

To those who viewed changing trends such as players querying refereeing decisions of no great importance, it was worth remembering rugby's image as a sport with high standards of player and crowd behaviour was worth preserving, not just for commercial reasons. Happily, the camaraderie of rugby's amateur era had not disappeared. Rival supporters didn't need to be separated and the Six Nations tournament remained a great social occasion with huge numbers of away supporters enjoying the experience of travelling to London, Cardiff, Rome, Dublin, Edinburgh and Paris to see their countries play.

While rugby union's players and followers retained many of game's amateur era values, the failure of the wealthy major rugby nations to aid the poverty stricken Pacific Islands of Fiji, Samoa and Tonga was a sorry story of self-interest, echoing attitudes of the distant past when rugby league was created because poorer players playing the sport were refused compensation for wages lost playing rugby.

In 1970, Fiji provided a spellbinding display of athleticism, defeating a star-studded Barbarians side that included the two great Welsh players JPR Williams and Phil Bennett, 29–9 at Gosforth. Decades later, the Fijians' ability as runners was reflected in their excellent Sevens record, highlighted by their winning the gold medal at the 2016 Rio de Janeiro Olympics blitzing Great Britain 43–7 in the final.

However, in the main 15-man game, the island nations generally found it hard to compete with major countries, with many of their players switching to other nations. But they had their successes. Samoa beat Wales four times while Tonga's six wins against Tier 1 nations included defeating the 2011 World Cup runners-up France 19–14 in their group match in Wellington.

Economic necessity prompted the large-scale exodus of gifted Pacific Islands rugby players to New Zealand, Australia and Europe to earn a living from the sport and so many of them played for their new countries with distinction. They could hardly be criticised as rugby mercenaries for leaving their homelands to earn a decent living that could benefit their families back home. As the formidable England No 8 Billy Vunipola said in an interview in September 2017: "The reason we came here to this vast country was we had nothing at home in Tonga. Back there we'd come home and eat breakfast leftovers, which were doughballs. It was not much of a life, which is why my granddad pushed us to come here."

Sadly, those running the wealthier rugby nations did little to help their poorer counterparts. This was highlighted when Fiji played England at Twickenham in an autumn international on 19 November 2016. While the South Pacific players were set to earn just £400 apiece from the game, the England players, including the Fijian-born wing Semesa Rokoduguni voted Man of the Match for his two-try role in the host nation's 58–15 victory, received £22,000 each. While the game generated some £10 million for the Rugby Football Union, Fiji were given a mere £75,000 as a "goodwill gesture" after their request for £150,000 of the match revenue was turned down.

Responding to adverse publicity over this Scrooge-like handout, RFU chief executive Ian Ritchie echoed memories of the 19th-century rugby establishment by showing a lofty disdain for the plight of the poorest rugby nations, stating: "It is not England's responsibility to help fund world rugby. We have absolutely no obligation to do anything."

Obviously, the term "moral obligation" had no place in the RFU's psyche. While host nations were not obliged to share any revenue with their opponents, Fiji had every right to feel they deserved a larger share of the profits for crossing the globe to play at Twickenham. The former Fiji Rugby Union chief executive Radrodro Tabualevu offered a damning take on Ritchie's patronising attitude: "When I went to Europe with the Fiji team, I was taken aback when I realised we didn't get a share of the gate takings. If the mission is to grow the game globally, we'd like to think we have a special part to play."

A year later, in 2017, Samoa seemed in an even worse place when their rugby union declared it was bankrupt while the team was touring Europe. The RFU paid their tour expenses but this was hardly that massive an act of largesse when the union's new chief executive Steve Brown had, a few weeks earlier, revealed the Game of Our Lives four-year masterplan, investing £443 million in expanding English rugby.

True, the three South Pacific nations were getting £20 million aid from World Rugby spread over a four-year cycle from 2016–2019. But alongside the RFU's huge income surplus, these figures seemed pretty minimalist.

The distorted logic that host nations should retain gate profits was hardly a fair return when the Pacific nations got no significant financial benefits on the rare occasions they were visited by major nations. When the All Blacks played a long-awaited Test in Samoa in 2015, it cost the island's RFU £200,000. If rugby administrators could have forgotten self-interest, the wealthier rugby nations could have aided the impoverished Pacific nations for the benefit of the Test rugby. Providing worthwhile Test match appearance fees and making the international qualification period ten years would have seen the island teams reflecting their true rugby prowess, with fewer of their major players changing allegiance to Tier 1 nations.

It was not only Pacific Island nations who were financially ambushed by the RFU. In November 2019, New Zealand played England at Twickenham, enabling the RFU to stage what was the richest match in rugby history, earning them an estimated £15 million, but there was no inclination to pass on any of these vast earnings to the visitors.

"They don't get a slice because that's not the way the market works," said RFU chief executive Steve Brown, an accountant by profession. "Steve Tew [New Zealand RFU chief executive] got a very nice slice from the Lions tour recently, so maybe I should phone him."

While it was true the existing system meant the New Zealand RFU kept all gate receipts when they hosted tour matches, their revenue was far below RFU levels. Despite fielding a Test side that had dominated World Rugby for over a decade, they needed the huge success of the 2017 Lions tour to get out of debt.

Sadly, financial imperatives increasingly held sway in the game's first 25 years of professionalism. This was confirmed when Australian Brett Gosper became chief executive officer of the IRB in 2012 before the World Rugby name change. An erudite, hugely successful marketing man, who spent 25 years advising major global companies, his mind was firmly anchored on making "brand rugby" a worldwide success. As he said in an interview in September 2016: "I am a comms person heart and soul but my views are always anchored in the reality of the business and the product truth behind a brand."

Gosper fielded questions on the state of the sport for an hour on the Sky Sports rugby programme *The Offload* on 8 November 2017, but surprisingly in a programme claiming to deal with the sport's major issues, no mention was even made of the injury crisis facing rugby. Just once was Gosper caught off-guard, when former Samoan international Dan Leo debated the vast player drain facing the Pacific Islands.

"I'm with Tonga in Limerick tonight," said Leo "and I've just spoken to the coaches who are really concerned that they've just lost 23 of their front-line high school players given scholarships provided they declare their allegiance to Japan."

No hint of condemnation or sense of regret regarding this event came from Gosper, who pointed out: "Ultimately it's the local union who has to decide if it's something which is good for their union or not."

But Leo contradicted this fence-sitting viewpoint. "That's not good enough," he told Gosper. "We need World Rugby to put their foot down and clamp down on people who are blatantly contravening World Rugby regulations." Gosper remained unmoved, unwilling to commit World Rugby to decisive action on the issue, stating: "We have to do that with the local union, we can't do that in isolation."

"Why not?" was the obvious retort. World Rugby was meant to be controlling the worldwide game and if that meant playing hardball with a union getting it wrong, then so be it.

Fears that rugby union would head the way of soccer in the future, with clubs wielding the power, were also voiced in the programme. Former England centre Will Greenwood suggested that the moneymen could turn the European Cup or the English Premiership into something bigger than international rugby, adding the somewhat weak, defeatist remark: "I'm not sure what you can actually do."

"I think you are right," replied Gosper, offering a disturbing insight into World Rugby's unwillingness to condemn the increasing power of clubs. "I think market forces will dictate what happens off the field."

Rugby union, for all its faults in the amateur era, at least did not place commercialism and marketing as a main priority. Bowing to the great god commercialism on this issue was something of an insult to the many thousands of rugby men who have devoted their lives to the game on and off the field, with no financial reward.

To those who argued every man has his price, tell that to the generations of gifted Welsh players who refused to opt for financial security by accepting tempting rugby league offers, because they did not want to desert the union game, their friends and their country.

The sorry state of French rugby offered a warning of an unhappy future for the game if commercialism rules. While the gruelling Top 14 club competition, with its long roll-call of heavily paid foreign imports in major sides, was apparently thriving, the national side had been in disarray. This was highlighted by the fact France could merely draw 23–23 with Japan in Paris on 25 November 2017. In the summer of that year came a sad reflection of priorities when France toured South Africa and lost the series 3–0, having played the first Test (a 37–14 defeat) without star players who were playing for Clermont or Toulon in the Top 14 final in Paris.

In 2019, Brett Gosper's view that market forces would control the sport in the future took a disturbing first step towards becoming a reality when the moneymen encircled rugby union. World Rugby was trying to get its much-criticised Nations Championship masterplan off the ground, hoping the prospect of £6.1 billion backing spread over 12 years from the Swiss-based sports marketing company Infront Sports & Media would sway the flawed scheme's many critics. Meanwhile, CVC Capital Partners, the Luxembourg-based private equity firm, may have failed in its bid to become the majority shareholder in the English Premiership. But it did succeed in getting a 27% stake in the business for more than £200 million. It then upped the raid on rugby's financial potential, offering £500 million for a 30% stake in the Six Nations, rugby's oldest tournament, which provided the hugely popular annual highlight in the northern hemisphere rugby calendar and had already been disfigured to a degree with fixture days and times geared to broadcasting revenue.

While the short-term benefits of financiers pouring millions into the sport may have seemed highly attractive, it was worth remembering these massive investments were hardly altruistic acts. They were intended to make money and player welfare would hardly rank as a major priority with investors seeking maximum profits from their ventures.

CVC had owned Formula One between 2006 and 2017 making vast profits from a sport with a huge worldwide interest. But their reign was not welcomed by all. In an article published on 10 September 2018, *Guardian* sportswriter Giles Richards offered rugby a sombre warning it might be receiving a hospital pass by allowing private equity a foothold in the sport. Describing CVC's control of Grand Prix racing from 2006–2017, he wrote: "There was the pursuit of profit at every possible level... It was a distasteful, cynical process that left Formula 1 tarnished." He pointed out that CVC's profit return was estimated up to £3.5 billion after spending £1.4 billion gaining a majority stake in the sport.

In June 2019, World Rugby's hugely flawed Nations Championship scheme was finally abandoned after the Six Nations tournament failed to back it, even though it would have boosted the revenues of the main unions taking part by some £15 million annually. World Rugby chairman Sir Bill Beaumont managed to portray this as the Home Union countries failing to support the global game, saying it was an unhappy outcome for the sport.

"World Rugby undertook this important project with the best interests of the global game at heart in line with our vision to grow the sport as a game for all," he said. "While we are naturally disappointed that a unanimous position on the Nations Championship could not be achieved among our unions, we remain fully committed to enhancing the meaning, value and opportunity of international rugby for the betterment of all unions."

This portrayal of World Rugby as trying to protect the game's best interests with this ill-conceived tournament hardly bore scrutiny. The Nations Championship would have seriously undermined the status of the World Cup, as its *raison d'être* was to ensure there was a competition annually to determine the leading Test nation. It would also have done nothing to lessen the unacceptable Test match treadmill inflicted on leading players. Its one virtue was the fact that it intended giving Tier 2 nations a chance to join rugby's top table, as the bottom sides in the six-strong northern and southern hemisphere leagues would have faced a relegation battle against the leading Tier 2 nation in their part of the world.

World Rugby making a stance on this issue smacked of hypocrisy, as throughout the game's professional era the IRB/World Rugby had effectively operated a financial apartheid, miserably failing to enable the hugely gifted but poverty-stricken Pacific Island nations to fulfil their potential at Test level while major nations were able to pillage their best players for decades. If the richer northern hemisphere rugby nations had given their poorer southern hemisphere opponents, New Zealand, South Africa, Australia and Argentina, as well as the Pacific Island nations, a reasonable share of Test gate money, it would have hugely benefitted the sport, and been fairer.

It didn't actually need a nations league to enable Tier 2 nations to join rugby's top table. The straightforward answer was for the Rugby Championship to match the Six Nations by expanding its format to six teams, so, say, Fiji and Japan would join New Zealand, South Africa, Australia and Argentina in the competition. And, as in the Six Nations, they would play each other just once a year. Then, when the two competitions ended, the bottom nation could face a relegation battle, having to win a home match against the leading Tier 2 side in their part of the world to remain in the major championship.

Imagine the huge interest if, as the 2018–2019 season drew to a close, Italy to avoid relegation from the Six Nations tournament had to win a one-off match in Rome against say Georgia? Or across the other side of the world, say Samoa had to beat Japan in Tokyo to gain a place in the Rugby Championship to play the leading southern hemisphere sides.

Test rugby remained a huge success in the professional era, despite the overcrowded international calendar. It seemed slightly illogical that rugby's administrators should surrender any part of their total control of this hugely profitable form of the game to marketing specialists. Agustín Pichot's argument that the Nations Championship was needed to reinvigorate

Test rugby was hugely misplaced. Rugby Tests had never been regarded as friendlies, despite their appeal being tarnished through the sheer volume of fixtures allowed to go unchecked in the professional era.

It was true, club rugby in England and France had dramatically risen in popularity in the professional era. When rugby union was a purely amateur sport there were invariably full houses at major grounds for internationals but audiences were generally small for club matches, except in Wales. After the game turned professional in 1995, English club rugby found a significant upsurge in attendance figures, with gates averaging 14,165 per match in the 2017–2018 season, but they hardly compared to the vast crowds regularly watching leading soccer clubs or rugby internationals.

Saracens offered a remarkable example of the changing face of English club rugby. Back in the early 1970s, they were a strong but unfashionable north London club, playing on a council pitch in Southgate with a solitary stand, usually watched by no more than a few hundred spectators. On 11 May 2019, they confirmed their status as the strongest club in the northern hemisphere, beating the Irish province Leinster 20–10 in the European Champions Cup final watched by 51,930 spectators at Newcastle United Football Club's stadium. Under the guidance of their outstanding director of rugby Mark McCall, they further emphasised their status as a great rugby side, irrespective of their financial chicanery, when they won the English Premiership title on a sunny Saturday afternoon at Twickenham on 1 June 2019 watched by a 75,329 crowd. Trailing 16–27 with 20 minutes play remaining, they staged a remarkable comeback to secure a thrilling 37–34 victory against a valiant Exeter side.

Four years earlier, on 28 March 2015, Saracens had set a world attendance record for a club rugby match when they beat Harlequins 42–14, watched by 84,068 spectators at Wembley Stadium, highlighting the sport's potential for expansion at club level. However, their home ground at Allianz Park in north-west London had a capacity of only 10,500, showing just how far rugby clubs trailed behind football clubs in live audience terms and stadium facilities.

For all the widespread publicity Saracens attracted and the hugely talented player base they provided for the England national side, the Premiership remained a bankrupt sporting model, paying inflated player salaries kept alive by the millionaire owners and the financial largesse of the RFU. Of the 12 Premiership clubs, Exeter Chiefs were the only side to make a profit in the 2017–2018 season.

The fact CVC viewed the Premiership as a shrewd future investment indicated its potential. But many would view it a sad day for the sport if club rugby was ever regarded as more important than Test rugby. Welcome though the huge increase in interest shown in club rugby in England was, equating club rugby with international rugby in terms of importance was sheer nonsense both in terms of finance generated and spectator interest.

On 23 February 2019, an estimated television audience of 8.9 million viewers, a vast audience for a sport that trails far behind soccer in appeal terms, watched Wales memorably defeat a much-vaunted England side 21–13 in their crucial Six Nations Championship encounter at the Principality Stadium in Cardiff. By comparison, Saracens' 37–24 Premiership final win against Exeter on 1 June had a peak audience of 297,000 viewers.

Rugby union retained the capacity to attract full houses at internationals when nothing more than pride was at stake, despite the fixtures overkill. The 82,149 capacity crowd that watched England play New Zealand at Twickenham on 10 November 2018 had highlighted the huge appeal generated when countries face each other less often – in this instance, for the first time in four years.

"Our research shows that we could have priced every

ticket at £195 and still sold out," said RFU chief executive Steven Brown, before his departure from the post. "As it is, we get 1.5–2.5 million inquiries for tickets for big matches at Twickenham."

Rugby union was popular enough to prosper with sensible bookkeeping, without needing to give financial enterprises influential roles and the chance to take a significant share of its profits. Or, indeed, without pricing tickets beyond the range of the average rugby supporter. Yet, despite being the game's most profitable union, the RFU still managed to get into financial trouble. Huge sums were spent financing the English Premiership to ensure clubs field mainly home-grown players rather than the foreign legions found in England's soccer clubs, and there was an overspend on the England national side's budget, including giving England players the extravagantly high figure of £24,000 a match for representing their country, to add to all their sponsorship perks.

The RFU had successfully transformed its Twickenham headquarters into an impressive 82,000-seater stadium with superb general facilities in the modern era. But it was decided to go a step further, spending a small fortune providing a corporate Valhalla in the ground's East Stand. Originally budgeted at £53.4 million, the East Stand development provided six floors of "creative event space" featuring lavish restaurants, conference rooms and bars. By the time it opened in 2018, the cost had risen to £80 million. Perhaps the RFU should have also included a casino for those indifferent to actually watching the rugby matches played in front of the stand.

Meanwhile, grassroots rugby, the lifeblood of the sport, fared less well, despite the need to halt the declining number of players. In November 2018, RFU chief executive Steve Brown resigned after just 14 months in the post amidst growing criticism of the RFU's financial state and Bill Sweeney, the British Olympic Association's successful chief executive, was appointed his successor. Before Brown's unexpected departure, the RFU announced a £30.9 million loss and 62 redundancies, with cuts in funding for grassroots rugby including the loss of highly regarded staff serving the amateur game.

In June 2019, former RFU chairman Martyn Thomas voiced his concerns that the disconnect between those running the game in England and the country's amateur clubs playing a vital role in ensuring a happy future for the sport was wider than ever. Interviewed by *The Rugby Paper*, he produced the disturbing verdict: "There was a longstanding culture of people in senior RFU posts who had played the game at whatever level and put back into the game. Now there seem to be faceless executives making sure that every door is shut to questions and queries. It's like the North Korean model of no one rocking the boat for fear of persecution."

A seemingly small incident in the autumn of 2018 illustrated the worrying trend that top-flight English club rugby was undermining the far more important Test scene. On 3 November, England won a narrow 12–11 victory against South Africa at Twickenham. Sitting in the stands viewing the game was the inspirational scrum-half Faf de Klerk, who had been a key figure in guiding his country South Africa to a 2–1 series win against England the previous summer as well as what should have been a remarkable two wins in the Rugby Championship against the All Blacks (New Zealand scored at the death to snatch a win in the second match).

The reason he was watching the game was his employers at the English Premiership club Sale, who did not have a fixture that day, would not release him for that game or, indeed, the other autumn internationals played by his country. Should the priorities of an average club playing in the English Premiership have taken priority over the needs of a great rugby nation?

In the most damaging example of the club v Test rugby conflict of interests, the treatment of the British & Irish Lions unhappily illustrated how commercialism and self-interest had increasingly replaced the values of rugby when it was a great amateur sport. Contrary to expectations, the Lions – a squad of the best rugby players in the UK and Ireland, given the honour of touring a major southern hemisphere nation every four years – became more popular than ever in the professional era. In 2005, when they toured New Zealand, Lions replica shirt sales reportedly exceeded 500,000, outstripping Real Madrid or Manchester United football clubs' figures. In 2009, more than 30,000 Britons travelled to South Africa to watch the Lions.

But the modern game saw Lions players become victims of an over-congested fixture list. In the summer of 2017, the Lions sought British rugby's Holy Grail, to repeat the historic achievement of the 1971 Lions by winning a Test series in New Zealand. Yet leading members of the tour party were handicapped by being unable to escape the club treadmill. The tour opened on 3 June, a week after many key tourists played in Aviva Premiership and Pro 12 finals at the end of a long, hard northern hemisphere season.

Saracens director of rugby Mark McCall, back in August 2016, voiced his view of the Lions tour: "It is ludicrous they are playing 10 games. No one talks about it because it's the Lions and the Lions are special." This complaint ignored the fact the Lions' true *raison d'être* was to play the leading sides in whichever country they are visiting. Playing 10 matches was hardly an endurance test compared to the 24-match schedule the 1971 Lions, all amateur players, played in New Zealand. What was "ludicrous" was the overlong club rugby programme wrecking the preparation schedule for leading players embarking on the experience of a lifetime.

As *Sunday Times* rugby correspondent Stephen Jones wrote before the 2017 Lions tour: "The British & Irish Lions are the biggest brand there is, the most glamorous and historic institution in rugby. Yet in a key sense no one cares. Many players will be battered and exhausted because the major finals of the home season will be played the day before they depart."

There was a straightforward solution to the problem. If clubs were unwilling to adjust the Premiership calendar once every four years for the benefit of the Lions tour, why couldn't they have put the cause of British rugby above self-interest and just given Lions coach Warren Gatland total control of the players once they were selected for the tour? Thus, if he so decided they would have missed club competition finals. In return, clubs would receive some of the considerable Lions tour profits as compensation for losing players during the club season climax.

McCall proved to be one of the game's great coaches, turning Saracens into a formidable force that ruled Europe, but did he really believe his club deserved priority above the Lions? No one would have disputed the English Premiership was a high standard competition, attracting widespread interest and providing an impressive array of talented players for the England national side. But the Lions were in a different league in playing, commercial, spectator and historic terms. By contrast, the Premiership was a league paying over-inflated player salaries with a far too cumbersome fixtures schedule.

What was more important to gifted England fly-half/centre Owen Farrell: winning yet another trophy playing for his club Saracens or his memorable feat of landing the crucial penalty in the third Test at Auckland that gave the 2017 Lions an unexpected drawn series, despite all the handicaps they had faced and against an All Blacks side hailed as the best sports side in the world?

But, astonishingly, with a new global season being planned, the projected 2021 Lions tour to South Africa was cut from six to five weeks with eight instead of 10 matches to avoid disrupting the English Premiership season.

"I fear for the future," was the reaction of the 2017 Lions manager John Spencer, the former England centre who was on the historic 1971 Lions tour. "What we have ended up with is crazy. In 2017 we were trimmed to the bare bones of a schedule. Players were falling asleep on the bus in that first week as they had no time to adapt to jet lag, let alone get to know each other."

By contrast, English Premiership Rugby chief executive Mark McCafferty had no qualms about the Lions tour being further undermined saying: "We said we were unhappy about the intensity of the schedule that had been signed up several years ago and it needs to change. To go through this kind of programme in the future is not feasible."

True rugby followers must have wondered what planet McCafferty inhabited. Amidst all the debate about their future, the achievement of the 2017 Lions to draw with New Zealand undoubtedly raised the profile of British rugby for the benefit of the sport generally, in a way no club could match. No doubt it was beyond McCafferty's comprehension, but it was the Premiership not the Lions that needed to change. The cumbersome league spread over 10 months, overpaying players, badly needed streamlining. No one would query the value of the English Premiership in providing an impressive roll-call of international standard players to represent England. But the downside of the 12-strong league was it involved a long drawn-out programme of 22 fiercely competitive club fixtures, plus a further one or two play-off matches for the top four sides to decide the league champions. Add the European Champions Cup fixtures, plus the yearly burden of a dozen Test fixtures and it was little surprise England's top players faced serious injury and burnout problems. While leading unions were unprepared to stop both touring and hosting tour Tests in the same year, neither did the English Premiership show any inclination to change its bulky playing model.

One solution would have been to create the equivalent of English cricket's two divisions by reducing club numbers to 10 in the Premiership and Championship and making the lower league a higher standard, with more funds, but this was obviously a heresy to the country's leading clubs. Alternatively, the Premiership could have matched its football equivalent by becoming a true league won by the table-topping club with no play-off matches. But common sense did not prevail. The Premiership, tired of one of their number being relegated each season, actually considered expanding its overlong season by making the league 13 rather than 12 sides.

With the league sensing its profile raised to new heights with CVC's financial involvement, it was no great surprise to find McCafferty stepping down as the Premiership CEO having created "a brilliant and captivating competition for all our fans" in his 14-year reign, to become an advisor with the private equity firm hunting down rugby as a potential financial bonanza.

The "captivating" tournament he had masterminded didn't look quite so "brilliant" when in January 2020 Saracens were relegated to the Championship whatever the results of their Premiership season. Inexplicably, after being fined £5.36 million and docked 35 points for ignoring salary cap rules in November 2019, they made no changes to their overblown salary structure, thus continuing the offence, and so were handed an automatic relegation penalty. The fact those controlling the Premiership had spent years failing to enforce their own salary cap regulations hardly said much for the way the Premiership was run.

Even harder to fathom than the salary cap scandal was how the Premiership could have equated itself anywhere near the British & Irish Lions in terms of importance. Purely in commercial terms, no other rugby side matched the appeal of the Lions. Ignoring the huge boost the tour gave the wider New Zealand economy with some 20,000 British and Irish rugby supporters travelling south of the equator to view matches, the 2017 Lions tour saw the New Zealand RFU make a profit of $33 million against a loss of $7 million in 2016. By contrast, in May 2018, Saracens, England's premier club side, were some

£45 million in the red and surviving through millionaire owner Nigel Wray's generosity and devotion to rugby.

In February 2020, the Premiership's stranglehold on the English game looked destined to reach a new level. Under the guidance of its new chief executive officer Bill Sweeney, the RFU inexplicably and without warning decided to halve the budget given to the Championship clubs in what was regarded as the feeder league, providing players for the Premiership. The 12 clubs in the Championship were told their budget of around £534,000 was being halved to a 2015 level of £288,000 per club for the 2020–21 season.

"This is a decision based on a principle of ensuring levels of investment are geared to a clear return on investment," was Sweeney's somewhat puzzling explanation for the draconian cut. The shocked reaction of the second-tier clubs was summed up by Nottingham chairman Alistair Bow with his withering condemnation: "Bill Sweeney may well go down as the man who ruined English rugby. The RFU have sold their soul to Premiership rugby and CVC."

The fact that the RFU had spent £80 million creating lavish corporate facilities in Twickenham's East Stand and were now reducing funding for England's 12 second-tier clubs was another clear signal that commercial considerations were being placed above the general welfare of the sport. Effectively, the financial bombshell was another significant step towards making the Premiership's ambition to end relegation and become a closed league no other club could join a reality. And the timing could hardly have been worse with players and staff negotiating their futures facing the prospect of redundancy rather than renewed contracts, with no prior warning.

"At 8.15am on Tuesday we received an email saying this is what they're doing – it was a bit like getting sacked by text," said Paul Durkin, chairman of third-placed Cornish Pirates. "We then met them in the afternoon. Every single club was shocked and we told Bill Sweeney and Conor O'Shea (RFU performance director) that effectively they had signed the death warrant of the second level of professional rugby in this country."

Faced with a tidal wave of protests, Sweeney backtracked a little on the original proposal and agreed to phase in the cut over two seasons.forgetting the wider implications of the decision, this hardly diminished the derision for the amateurish autocratic way the RFU had handled the whole issue.

The Rugby Football Union may no longer have controlled the sport in the professional era, but it remained hugely influential. However, it was a sad state of affairs when the RFU failed to reflect their past role as guardians of the sport by failing to advocate reversing the many wrong turns taken by rugby union in the first 25 years of the professional era.

The fact the Premiership had been allowed to jeopardise the future of the British & Irish Lions tours and the financial cutbacks and staff redundancies forced upon the second tier of professional rugby and grassroots rugby in England by the world's most affluent rugby union offered a poor reflection of the sport's changing priorities.

CHAPTER 8

# The Good and the Bad – The 2019 World Cup

*With all the "fantastic technology" available, why did World Rugby turn a Nelsonian blind eye to the fact so many of its own laws were being consistently ignored by players?*

THE GREAT SUCCESS of the 2019 World Cup in Japan highlighted both the huge appeal of the game of rugby union as a spectator sport and also its shortcomings which severely limited its scope for expansion as a game enjoyed by players in the professional era.

The host country's success winning all their group matches while defeating Tier 1 nations Ireland (19–12) and Scotland (28–21) ignited the tournament before their 26–3 quarter-final defeat against the powerful South Africans. In a country with a 126 million population, the television audience for Japan's emotionally charged victory against Scotland after Typhoon Hagibis had claimed more than 80 lives reached a remarkable viewing peak of 54.8 million.

But while more than half the country's population witnessed their countrymen defeat a major rugby nation, the reality was this famous victory was unlikely to produce a significant expansion of the game in its existing form in Japan.

We were hardly in new territory in 2019 as World Rugby's failure to make the game significantly safer offered a parallel to the 2015 World Cup. The prediction from *The Times* chief sports writer Matt Dickinson that the unquestioned success of the 2015 event hosted by England was unlikely to herald hordes of newcomers taking to playing rugby proved all too true. Dickinson had ominously predicted the bone-jarring hits were not a selling point for "fretting mothers" and he was right. The worrying decline in playing numbers of youngsters in major rugby countries such as England, Wales and even New Zealand showed the reality facing the sport.

In 2019, in the wake of Japan's inspirational World Cup campaign, BBC Radio 5 Live commentator Andrew Cotter echoed the same pessimism voiced by Dickinson four years earlier, saying: "I've been chatting to Japanese people and asking where does rugby sit in the firmament and it's actually still not that high. They like watching rugby but it's still not a massive sport. Ultimately that lack of bulk is still going to cost them at the very highest level. They've shown that with their speed and their skill they can get to a certain point but it's just a very hard game to play if you're always on the back foot because of the power game."

The ball-playing skills of the Japanese were universally admired during the World Cup. But under the game's existing laws they were outplayed by the hugely physical South African side in the quarter-final as the Springboks were able to pick up and drive into their opponents time and time again without losing possession.

In its population of 126 million, Japan had 295,939 rugby players. But even taking the obvious step of ending the country's isolation from rugby's top table by including Japan and also Fiji in the Rugby Championship, it was unlikely a country where the average height was just 5ft 2in would ever win the World Cup while the sport's power/skill ratio remained so distorted.

At the World Cup in Japan, World Rugby with commendable decisiveness finally decided on a zero-tolerance approach to players hitting opponents' necks or heads with tackles and shoulder-charging opponents with no-arms tackles. After the first few days of the tournament, the unprecedented step of issuing a statement criticising refereeing standards was taken, following a meeting of the referees, touch judges and TMOs with Alain Rolland, World Rugby's referee chief. After that meeting, rugby's main administrative body announced: "Following the usual review of matches, the match officials team recognise that performances over the opening weekend were not consistently of the standards set by World Rugby and themselves, but World Rugby is confident of the highest standards of officiating moving forward."

The chief incident that resulted in the statement was the Australian winger Reece Hodge hitting Peceli Yato with a dangerous tackle that forced the key Fijian player to leave the field with the match in the balance on the second day of the tournament. Hodge was not punished for the offence during the game the Australians went on to win 39–21. It was scant consolation for the South Pacific team that he was later given a three-match ban after being cited for his no-arms tackle.

Bizarre though the statement may have seemed, publicly voicing criticism of the refereeing at such an early stage in the tournament, it had the great merit that for once World Rugby was really making player welfare a main priority in prevention terms. The fact referees were told to sharpen up their act made headline news, sending a clear message to players they would now be off the field for 10 minutes in the sin bin or get a red card for making dangerous tackles. Offences continued on a lesser scale after the warning and the fact the tournament produced eight red cards demonstrated the traditional rugby tackle was preferable to a high tackle that could easily end up making contact with an opponent's neck or head.

Players could hardly complain about the new approach, as Rolland had warned days before the tournament started that red and yellow cards would be brandished without hesitation for illegal high tackles. Just before the final was played, World

Rugby hailed the success of its "high tackle sanction framework" operated during the tournament, looking to protect players by getting tackles lower.

"Innovative Rugby World Cup 2019 drives best-ever player welfare outcomes" was the eye-catching headline conjured by the organisation's Dublin-based media office on the World Rugby website. The statistics showed concussion rates at RWC 2019 had reduced by 35% when compared to 2018–19 elite competition levels and 12% when compared with Rugby World Cup 2015. The figures were 10.5 concussions per 1,000 player hours in RWC 2019 compared with 12.5 concussions per 1,000 player hours in RWC 2015, while the elite competition levels in the 2018–19 period were 17 concussion incidents per 1,000 player hours.

World Rugby chairman Sir Bill Beaumont, hailing this success, said: "Our commitment to player welfare is unwavering and a core pillar of our strategies is to reduce injuries. It is highly encouraging that Rugby World Cup 2019 has demonstrated extremely positive outcomes in this priority area."

His chief medical officer Dr Martin Raftery, was equally enthusiastic: "Our role is to ensure that we can provide the best possible standard of care to our players, driven by an evidence-based approach. At this tournament, and in the Tests since May, we have been looking to protect players by changing culture and getting the tackler lower. These very positive outcomes suggest that the teams have embraced the challenge and that risk has lowered at this Rugby World Cup, which is very encouraging."

However, the welcome reduction in concussion injuries in Japan through World Rugby's "zero-tolerance" approach to dangerous high tackles was long overdue. The reality was the administrators had finally merely fulfilled their promise to effectively enforce their own existing law relating to dangerous tackles. What happened in the 2019 World Cup was hardly "innovative" as it was merely a repeat of a directive made three years earlier stating dangerous tackles would be effectively punished. At the end of 2016, World Rugby announced from 3 January 2017 there would be a "zero-tolerance approach" with referees instructed to issue yellow or red cards to players making reckless tackles that hit the neck or head area. The result was a spate of yellow and red cards for blatantly dangerous tackles and a major debate with some making the absurd claim the game had "gone soft". But it took another three years and the 2019 World Cup to finally see a true zero-tolerance policy ruthlessly adopted.

In fact, back in November 2010 the IRB Board medical conference held in London had recognised the failure in policing the tackle law effectively, stating players guilty of making dangerous tackles were "not being suitably sanctioned". A study in England had reached the somewhat obvious conclusion that "stricter implementation of the laws of rugby relating to collisions and tackles above the line of the shoulder may reduce the number of head/neck injuries". However, this IRB conference could hardly be accused of tackling the problem decisively, as the result of its deliberations was a lukewarm memorandum stating: "An illegal high tackle involving a stiff arm or swinging arm to the head of the opponent, with no regard to the player's safety, bears all the hallmarks of an action which should result in a red card or a yellow card being seriously considered."

"Seriously considering" sending offenders off the field was no great deterrent and the fact it took nine years before the IRB's successor, World Rugby, finally adopted a long overdue, true zero-tolerance policy in Japan was hardly a reflection of good governance.

The statistics produced hailing the success of this initiative offered an interesting contradiction of World Rugby's oft-repeated claim their player welfare policies were working. The fact the 12.5 concussions per 1,000 player hours recorded for the 2015 World Cup had risen steeply to 17 concussions per

1,000 player hours in elite competitions such as the Six Nations in the 2018–19 period hardly indicated the game's injury crisis was under control. World Rugby's commitment to taking care of concussed players was praiseworthy but what should have been regarded as unacceptable was their blatant inability to both realise and tackle the prime causes of an unsustainable injury crisis.

Sheltering behind platitudes such as "player welfare" being their main priority and a commitment to "evidence-based research" failed to disguise the unwelcome reality that realistic solutions to the game's problems frequently voiced publicly by leading media figures, famous ex-internationals and eminent medics (see the Quotes for Change section at the start of this book) were ignored for years by the IRB/World Rugby.

The 2019 World Cup also found Scotland embroiled in another unhappy controversy that dented the game's image as a sport with decent values. After their controversial exit from the 2015 World Cup at the quarter-final stage, they again made headline news when Scottish Rugby chief executive Mark Dodson threatened to sue the 2019 oganisers if his country's fixture with Japan was cancelled rather than postponed because of the Typhoon Hagibis disaster. In the end the game was played and an inspirational Japanese performance knocked Scotland out of the tournament, then Scottish Rugby were fined £70,000 for Dodson's outburst against the tournament organisers.

Despite being disrupted by the strongest typhoon to hit Japan for decades, no one would question the 2019 World Cup was a huge success. Japan's heady triumph, beating two major nations by playing spectacular running rugby, England's epic 19–7 semi-final victory against the much-vaunted All Blacks and South Africa's 32–12 victory in the final, comprehensively defeating the nation who created the sport with a compelling mix of sheer power and skill, were all memorable highlights, superbly televised. More importantly, the event echoed that evocative 1967 tribute to the game from New Zealand chief justice Sir Richard Wild: "It treats every man as equal from whatever background he comes from. There's no yielding to status in a rugby tackle, there's no privilege in a scrum."

Rugby's virtues as a sport transcending race and class were epitomised when the first black South African rugby captain, Siya Kolisi, raised in a poverty-stricken township, held the World Cup aloft. He was watched by Afrikaner Rassie Erasmus, the impressive Springboks coach who had appointed him 18 months earlier to lead his country in what had been a white man's sport, until the racial injustices of South Africa were effectively attacked by the Anti-Apartheid Movement.

This was also the first time rugby's most important tournament had been staged by a minor rugby nation. Beaumont justifiably voiced the view what happened in Japan "will be remembered as probably the greatest World Cup". The fact it was a genuine contest, ending New Zealand's dominance of the global scene with many memorable rugby games, was backed by the huge interest in the tournament. World Rugby could rightly claim credit for choosing Japan as hosts. Stadiums were filled to 99% capacity with 1.84 million tickets sold, while the host nation's victory over Scotland attracted that record domestic television audience of 54.8 million. This was a staggering figure when you remember 12.8 million UK viewers watched England's defeat in the final. In addition, the tournament generated 1.7 billion video views of match action online.

However, what was disturbing was World Rugby's failure to realise the game needed to be made safer, to take advantage of the massive opportunity to expand the game which had been provided by the vast interest generated by events in Japan. Complacently ignoring reality was reflected in the way Beaumont and Dr Raftery hailed the high tackle initiative in Japan as a major triumph and that media office claim the tournament had driven the "best-ever player outcomes".

161

The fact Wales endured an injury crisis reaching epidemic proportions as the tournament drew to a close vividly illustrated the problem that the game's emphasis on collision was still producing an unsustainable level of injuries that totally contradicted the player welfare claim.

Absent from Japan was the inspirational Welsh captain Sam Warburton, who had led the British & Irish Lions on two successful tours, as at the relatively young age of 29, in July 2018, he had retired, with a daunting list of major injuries ending his playing career. Also absent from the squad sent to Japan were Toby Faletau, the world-class No 8 ruled out with a collarbone injury, and first choice fly-half Gareth Anscombe, who suffered a severe knee injury playing England in a warm-up match before the flight to Asia.

In Japan, matters got progressively worse. Wales suffered two major blows when their best attacking player Liam Williams, with an ankle injury, and dynamic back row forward Josh Navidi, with a hamstring injury, found their tournaments at an end before the crucial semi-final against South Africa. To their great credit, Wales narrowly lost this match against the eventual trophy winners 19–16 after the scores were level at 16–16 in the closing stages. Their centres Jonathan Davies and Hadleigh Parkes both played that match with lingering injuries while the Welsh were further handicapped when prop Tomas Francis, with a painful shoulder injury, and their formidable winger George North, with a pulled hamstring, both departed the field for good before half-time.

By the time Wales understandably lost their final play-off match versus the formidable All Blacks by 40–17, the squad's injury toll had reached epidemic proportions. Their courageous full-back Leigh Halfpenny (concussion) and the promising flanker Aaron Wainwright (hamstring) had joined Francis and North on the casualty list, missing the game which ended coach Warren Gatland's much praised 12-year reign as Welsh coach.

While concussion remained the game's major injury concern as brain damage is a hugely emotive subject, rugby's injury crisis spanned a far wider spectrum, as the Welsh injury toll showed. However, illegal high tackles were far from the sole cause of concussion. In the World Cup final, England's promising prop Kyle Sinckler sadly left the field for good after just two minutes play after he was knocked out when hit by team colleague Maro Itoje's elbow as the two players double tackled an opponent entirely legally.

The wealth of favourable publicity from the 2019 World Cup obscured the fact that rugby faced an uncertain future. Reflecting on rugby's first 25 years of professionalism, the end of amateurism resulted in many gains for the sport. But the sad reality was the misguided efforts of IRB/World Rugby to make rugby more free-flowing had turned rugby union into a dangerous sport. However large and strong players became by bulking up in the gym and conditioning their bodies, it did not prevent them constantly breaking down.

In 2020, two of the northern hemisphere's most powerful players evidenced the price of being a leading rugby union professional in the modern game. Toby Faletau returned to the Welsh side for the Six Nations tournament after two arm fractures and a broken collarbone had kept him out of Test rugby for nearly two years. By contrast England No 8 Billy Vunipola missed the 2020 Six Nations after suffering a broken arm playing against Racing 92 in January. It was the fourth arm fracture the 27-year-old had suffered in his career.

Injuries were not the only unfortunate by-product of rugby's undue emphasis on confrontation. The fact South Africa were able to shut Japan out of their quarter-final with their huge pack preventing their opponents getting any decent possession also showed how the brawn/skill ratio had escalated out of proportion in the modern game, endangering the sport's future expansion.

The final illustrated that it was not only the smaller sides that suffered from ill-advised law changes. Scrum dominance proved the key to South Africa's success as the misguided decision to end the scrum as a hooking contest meant England had no way of avoiding giving away penalties after being outshoved and outmanoeuvred by the formidable Springboks eight.

Having already defeated Wales in a monotonous kick-fest in their semi-final, South Africa deservedly won the trophy, showing a compelling mix of power and skill against an England side that had knocked the All Blacks out of the tournament.

While rugby's tradition as a game for all sizes was often perceived as ending in the modern era, the decisive role played by the two smallest players on the field, each just 5ft 7in tall, in the final showed that exceptional skill could still reign above power. The heartbeat of the South African side was the inspirational scrum-half Faf de Klerk while victory was sealed when the dynamic winger Cheslin Kolbe, with a blistering change of direction, left five England defenders in his wake in an electrifying 40-metre sprint to the try line.

Japan 2019 also showed how 25 years of professionalism had failed to significantly expand rugby's band of leading nations. In 1995 in Paris, the Welsh QC Vernon Pugh, the IRB reformer, announced that rugby would finally embrace professionalism, ending its amateur status. Pugh's vision of a worldwide expansion of the sport did not come to pass, largely through the hugely damaging three-year residency rule resulting in leading South Pacific island players switching their allegiance to the affluent major rugby nations and the financial apartheid operated by the wealthier rugby unions unwilling to part with gate money.

Of the 48 Pacific Island players featuring in the 2019–20 English Premiership, only 29 represented Fiji, Samoa and Tonga while the remainder had been captured by Tier 1 nations.

During the 2019 World Cup, leading British rugby writer

Brendan Gallagher had no difficulty selecting a hugely gifted XV consisting of Pacific Island exiles playing for France, Australia, New Zealand and Japan in the tournament.

Those handling rugby's destiny deserved condemnation for stubbornly ignoring the calls for change and betraying the game's heritage by their meek tolerance of the fact it had become too collision-based. Yet no one suggested that Brett Gosper, Bill Beaumont, John Jeffrey and Dr Martin Raftery should be replaced.

The disturbing result of decades of indecisiveness was the emergence of a generation of rugby players and spectators regarding the huge tackle and injury count in the modern game as the norm. While leading modern players occasionally voiced the reality of playing an injury-ridden sport, it was hardly in their interests to criticise the way the game that provided them with a career and fame was run.

However, in August 2019, the universally admired former Wales and British & Irish Lions captain Sam Warburton broke ranks in his autobiography *Open Side*, voicing the lurid prediction that a professional player would die in front of television cameras in a major match "if something isn't done soon". The legacy of a career that saw him forced to retire at the relatively young age of 29 as his body "just couldn't take any more" made gruesome reading: "I've got a pin in my left shoulder, another pin in my right shoulder, a plate in my jaw and another in my eye socket."

Those calling for rugby to be made a safer game with less physical contact were often accused of trying to make the sport "soft". This accusation could hardly be levelled at Warburton. A player in the warrior class who once played on in a Test with a broken jaw, he never complained about the physical price he paid for his tackling ability and skill at winning turnover ball at the breakdown, that earned his reputation as one of the great openside wing forwards of the modern era.

While his verdict, "I'm one of the lucky ones – people

are dying on rugby pitches" ranked as an over-dramatic, somewhat crude portrayal of the risks of playing rugby, it was no exaggeration that the perception it had become a dangerous sport was becoming more and more prevalent. In his chapter titled 'The Future of the Game', he narrated the changes he would make if he was the World Rugby supremo with *carte blanche* to do as he wished.

Warburton was far too young to have appreciated in rugby's amateur era teams were unable to hold onto the ball for phase after phase continually crashing into opponents as the law forbidding a tackled player from manhandling the ball ensured a true contest for possession at the breakdown. And he advocated no law changes that restored a true contest at the breakdown, ending brick wall rugby.

But, with commendable clarity he did call for moves to end the unsustainable treadmill facing leading players by imposing a limit of 25 games per season and also limiting full contact training, a significant source of injuries, to just 10 minutes per week. Lest anyone thought he was undervaluing the physical aspects of rugby union, he added, "I didn't like contact in training, not because I didn't like tackling – I loved tackling – but I wanted to protect myself so I could be as physical as possible on a weekend."

He also echoed the oft-repeated but bizarrely ignored call for World Rugby to ensure the tackle area was a safer place by simply strictly enforcing its own law forbidding players to crash into opponents at the breakdown without binding onto a team colleague or opposition player. Warburton also recommended the most obvious route to making rugby a safer sport by simply getting rid of impact subs but only on a limited scale. Calling for a six-player subs bench rather than eight players able to take the field as replacements he added: "It would be nice to go back to the old amateur ethos of only bringing on a sub for injury, but let's be honest, in the professional game that is never going to happen."

Why on earth not? Was not the argument that bringing on fresh players was wrong from both a rugby and medical point of view, voiced by leading rugby figures for more than a decade, valid? Impact players didn't deserve to be regarded as an essential feature of the game of rugby union or part of the sport's heritage. Indeed, the reverse was true, for they transformed a 15-man sport into a 23-man game with a measure hijacked from rugby league in 1996, initially with five replacements allowed for tactical reasons. The argument that professional players would abuse an injury-only subs law was no reason to continue the damage being done to the game by allowing sides to replace more than half their team during a match.

Reverting to a four-man, injury-only subs bench would have made a significant difference in terms of player safety as well as making the game less complex even if it was abused. Remember also, pretending to be injured was far from a straightforward process. In 2009, the notorious Bloodgate Scandal involving Harlequins showed the heavy price that could be paid for a club faking an injury to get a player replaced.

Aside from being in direct contact with players during the half-time stoppage, how could a coach who was willing to risk his career taking this route, instruct a player to go down injured while the game was being played? Rugby is fond of claiming the moral high ground over footballers who dive to earn penalties. Would pretending you were injured as you were being outplayed be any less reprehensible?

Neither was faking injury a simple process even if it remained undetected initially. In the 2019 World Cup final in Japan, a key to South Africa's victory was their scrum dominance after England's tighthead prop Kyle Sinckler left the field concussed in the opening minutes of the match. It was not difficult to imagine the media mayhem that would have erupted had his troubled replacement Dan Cole departed the field injured, resulting in the game being played with uncontested scrums that would have negated South Africa's crucial ability to win scrum penalties.

As captain of two hugely successful Lions tours, Warburton recognised international rugby was the sport's showpiece, providing the bulk of the sport's revenue, and he called for all regular international players to be centrally contracted. The English Premiership with its over-inflated view of its own importance reflected in its disdainful treatment of the Lions tour concept has fought this viewpoint. But as Warburton said: "Rugby union isn't football where at least the more successful clubs have followings as large and rabid as national teams. In any club-country debate, country has to come first."

However, World Rugby had not been prepared to get involved in a club/country battleground by ending the huge match treadmill facing leading players, despite its claim player welfare was its main priority. Its weak governance of the game was sadly characterised by a reluctance to do anything to upset the unions and clubs. So, the match treadmill facing leading players continued, with commercial priorities more important than player welfare. No one dared contemplate the obvious route to countering losing match revenue: simply pay players less in a sport where the salary structure had become unrealistically inflated. In fact, rather than cutting the Test rugby overload facing players, World Rugby in 2019, seduced by that £6.1 billion sponsorship offer from Infront Sports & Media, tried unsuccessfully to promote a misguided Nations Championship that would have increased player pressures and done nothing to reduce the overloaded Test fixtures list.

In 2020, Beaumont and Pichot battling against each other in the election for World Rugby chairman, when the Englishman's initial four-year tenure ended, both advocated their holy grail of transforming the rugby calendar creating a "global game". In April 2020, with the world embroiled in the Covid-19 virus crisis and sport in complete halt mode, Stuart Barnes, the former England and Bath fly-half turned rugby columnist, produced a withering attack of the concept of a global game with a Nations League for Test rugby. With commendable clarity, he outlined rugby union's route to a successful future that didn't revolve around commercialism and private equity investment.

In a feature in *The Times* newspaper headlined "Forget growing the game – shrink it for quality", Barnes attacked World Rugby's timid governance of the sport and outlined his CTC (Cut The Crap) masterplan: "The number of games would be determined by a governing body that needs to start governing if it is not to be swept away as an irrelevance of a bygone age."

He advocated ending the cumbersome English Premiership season by cutting the league from 12 to 10 clubs with no play-off system. This would have meant the title winner would have played 18 rather than 24 games and made avoiding club and country clashes easier. The other benefits listed by Barnes were: "Less is more. Fewer matches means a need for fewer players. The pool of player talent will be deepened with only the very best making the grade.

"Players are unlikely to earn the same salaries they were paid before coronavirus revealed the substantial weakness of the game's business model. With fewer players the fear of massive wage cuts and substantial salary-capping can be moderated. This proposal does not envisage big as beautiful and it sees rugby as sanity in diminution."

In a perceptive analysis of World Rugby's misguided obsession with creating "a global game", Barnes, in a follow-up feature headlined "Return rugby to its touring roots" called for rugby tours to regain their traditional status as an integral part of the sport's appeal, writing: "Globalised rugby means jetting all over the world. No talk of rationing air miles from Beaumont or Pichot. Familiarity breeds contempt. Television is a problem. It feeds our addiction for live sport and their addiction for sponsorship and revenue. It sucks the soul out of sport. Converting the November internationals into part of a world league as broadcasters want would do long-term damage to the World Cup. There would come a time when we would stop noticing the difference between World Cup Champions and World League winners, or whatever you want to name the Never-Ending League.

"There is an alternative. It is called touring. The November series should be about three-Test tours. Three internationals, a series at stake. A once-in-six-years chance to win a home series against South Africa. That has heft.

"Rugby's roots are in touring. The Lions, the epic South Africa versus New Zealand tours of old. Even the recent England 3–0 win in Australia. A 'first ever'. How England's fans crowed. History matters to the rugby fan."

Those who regarded the views of Barnes as a misguided throwback to rugby's amateur past should have noted arguably the greatest success story of the professional era, the British & Irish Lions tour. In the amateur era, the tours south of the equator involving the leading players in the Home Nations attracted huge interest. Remarkably more than 800,000 spectators in a country with a population of less than 2.5 million watched the 1959 Lions play 25 matches in New Zealand.

With the advent of mass air travel, the Lions became more popular than ever in the professional era with vast numbers of British and Irish supporters travelling south of the equator to watch matches. In 2009 it was calculated upwards of 30,000 British supporters travelled 6,000 miles to watch the Lions play in South Africa while in 2017 an estimated 20,000 made the far longer journey to the other side of the world to see the 2017 Lions play in New Zealand.

In purely commercial terms, those 2017 Lions not only transformed the finances of the host union but gave a huge lift to the New Zealand economy with the tourism boost.

Ironically, considering it more than met the commercial imperatives of the professional era, that Lions tour was fighting for survival as the English Premiership, whose television audiences were tiny compared to football or Test rugby, refused to cut their fixtures schedule for the benefit of the far more important Lions tours taking place once every four years. The ridiculous result was leading English players found themselves playing a Premiership final a day before the Lions party were due to fly from the UK.

Even more baffling was the fact in the amateur era players interrupted their careers for as long as three months for the honour of representing the Lions, often at considerable financial cost. But in the professional era when players are paid to play rugby, the Lions tours were drastically cut in size, losing their role as ambassadors for the sport with players visiting schools and attending functions, increasing the popularity of the sport.

In 2017, the Lions achieved the epic feat of drawing a Test series 1–1 with the world champions, New Zealand, despite the tour schedule of 10 games in the space of six weeks limiting the opportunity for what was basically a scratch side, unused to playing with each other, to fulfil its considerable potential. By contrast, the 1971 Lions tour lasted three months.

Worse was to follow. The inexplicable treatment of the Lions as an irritating intrusion claiming the services of leading English Premiership players continued with the planned 2021 tour to take on the world champions South Africa, being cut to eight games spread over five weeks. As the former Wales fly-half Phil Bennett, star of the undefeated 1974 Lions tour in South Africa, said: "It's going to be very tough for them to beat the world champions with so few warm-up games. The English players could be playing in the Premiership final on the Saturday and then on the Monday flying out to play for the Lions."

But far more worrying than misplaced strategic decisions was the fact World Rugby were not willing to make the on-field reforms needed to make the game safer. The downsides that the changes needed would have meant player and coach redundancies and disgruntled clubs and countries undertaking major tactical changes were far outweighed by the fact rugby union would have become a safer, far less complex and more appealing sport, with increased sponsorship benefits.

A major problem was the obsession with researching the nature of rugby injuries and a seeming acceptance of the misconception that bigger players inevitably meant more injuries. The nature of injuries in the professional era were much the same as those in the amateur era. The problem was the injury-count inevitably rose because the collision count became so much higher. Did anybody seriously believe injury levels would have remained at a relatively low level in the 20th century when players were smaller if tackle rates involving players crashing into each other had been three times higher? Over a century, player sizes significantly increased when the game was amateur but no one raised concerns that injury levels were increasing too.

If World Rugby felt unable to make the crucial decision to go back to the old tackle law, ending tackled players handling the ball, there was a simple way of ending union sides holding onto the ball for phase after phase and employing the monotonous pick-and-go tactic close to the try line. Just adopt the rugby league six tackle law. Ironically this league law would have made rugby union less, not more, like rugby league. Unlike the 13-man code, play would have continued at the breakdown for five tackles with possession only being surrendered with the sixth tackle handing the opposition the put-in at a scrum. The end result would have been that sides unable to continually hold onto the ball for tackle after tackle would have resorted to evasion, offloads and kicking skills to outwit opponents.

The most damning consequence of IRB/World Rugby failing to enforce its own laws was the end of one of the most distinctive features of rugby union that made it different to every other sport – the art of hooking.

"The aim is to promote a fair contest for possession while also giving an advantage to the team putting the ball into the scrum," was the laughable justification for the 2017 law change effectively legalising what had always been a crooked scrum feed. How could it be deemed a fair contest when the opposition had zero chance of hooking the ball as it was being fed directly to the opposing set of forwards?

It was the ultimate irony in the professional era, with the hugely sophisticated television coverage with the TMOs able to view video replays of incidents and the 10-minute sin bin providing a hugely effective deterrent, World Rugby was reluctant to rigidly enforce all the laws of the game, fearful play would be interrupted by endless stoppages. The reality, as shown by the zero-tolerance policy finally adopted for the high tackle law in the 2019 World Cup, was players would abide by the laws rather than spend 10 minutes in the sin bin or have their game ended with a red card.

Before the 2019 World Cup, John Jeffrey, chairman of World Rugby's match official selection committee, stated: "The TMO is a part of the match officials team and the fantastic technology available is a tool to be used in the making of key decisions during matches. The TMO process is used to make sure the correct calls are made to protect the integrity of the game."

One was left wondering with all the "fantastic technology" available, why did World Rugby turn a Nelsonian blind eye to the fact so many of its own laws were being consistently ignored by players? Even more disturbing than the game's laws not being enforced was the fact you found referees constantly warning players to obey the laws of the game. Why should they have been obliged to advise professional players who should know the rules of the sport they were playing to remain onside or cease trying to grab the ball at the breakdown?

Another bizarre feature of the modern game perplexing many was the fact when the referee shouted "Ball is available" at the breakdown, the scrum-half was able to hover over the ball posing for five seconds before sending a box kick skywards.

In January 2020, World Rugby chairman Sir Bill Beaumont, interviewed by the *Daily Telegraph*'s chief rugby correspondent Gavin Mairs, finally showed a welcome change of direction by backing a trial law banning impact subs.

"I do worry it has become a game for big people," said Beaumont.

But this was hardly a Road to Damascus conversion, for any idea that the change would come anytime soon was dispelled by Beaumont's indecisiveness that characterised World Rugby's inability to make a decision that would be opposed by clubs, coaches or unions.

"It is an idea and we need to look at it in a controlled manner as opposed to an emotional one or someone writing on the back of a fag packet. We can only do it by trialling it at the top level in conjunction with the medics. But we have to ensure we don't become reckless in what we do."

CHAPTER 9

# The End of an Era – 27 August 2020

*"We have to stand up to aggressive commercial concerns who want to put money solely in the pockets of the few."*

MAJOR ANNIVERSARIES ARE normally regarded as events to be celebrated but the 25th anniversary of rugby union's historic decision to end amateurism on 27 August 2020 merited no great fanfare.

After 25 years of professionalism, rugby was once again a sport at the crossroads with unhappy echoes of the past facing it. On Sunday, 27 August 1995, after a three-day meeting of the International Rugby Board in Paris, the pioneering Welsh rugby administrator Vernon Pugh had announced union players would be paid for the first time. This unexpected decision avoided the southern hemisphere giants, South Africa, New Zealand and Australia, creating a professional rugby circus backed by Rupert Murdoch's News International global media organisation. Pugh persuaded the IRB delegates they had no choice but to vote for radical change. Even the most diehard defender of amateurism realised professionalism was preferable to civil war.

Pugh, who headed the working party masterminding the reform, had no regrets about the decision to make rugby union an open sport so players could be paid for filling Test stadiums around the world, stating later: "If we had not taken that decision then, I have no doubt the game would have disintegrated. We had to acknowledge the changes which had taken place. The southern hemisphere had put building blocks in place for professionalism. There was no point in fiddling about. It was too late for evolution."

A quarter of a century later, the financial equation was somewhat different, with the southern hemisphere nations seeking a new global calendar backed by private equity finance so they could secure greater financial parity with the wealthier northern hemisphere nations controlling the sport. Then, in March 2020, rugby's problems with its injury crisis, overspending, conflicting interests and overloaded fixture list were compounded when the worldwide Covid-19 virus crisis brought all sport to a halt, decimating the game's finances when matches ceased.

Sadly, since his early death aged just 57 in 2003, there had been no one matching Pugh's sharp intellect and decisiveness to end the injury crisis blighting the game and ensure commercialism didn't override the game's best interests in the second decade of the 21st century.

Like those two other great post-war Welsh rugby visionaries Carwyn James and John Dawes, Pugh was the son of a coalminer, born in the Valleys, attending the University College of Wales, Aberystwyth. He went on to qualify as a barrister after studying law at Cambridge University, later becoming a QC specialising in planning and environmental law. A later invitation to become a high court judge was turned down as he preferred to be shaping the future of rugby.

His ascent to the top of rugby's administrative ranks was swift and by a quirk of fate. In 1989, Pugh's reputation as a respected barrister heavily involved with Cardiff Harlequins, one of the city's junior rugby clubs, as a coach, resulted in the Welsh Rugby Union asking him to compile a report on the Welsh involvement in the South African Rugby Board's centenary celebrations in 1989. Ten leading Welsh internationals and six Welsh Rugby Football Union officials took part in the controversial tour that involved two World XV matches versus the Springboks even though the event had not been sanctioned by their Welsh RFU because South Africa's system of apartheid was still in place. His report offered early evidence that Pugh was not afraid of conflict for it advocated wholesale reform of the Welsh RFU, judging the union ill-equipped to run the sport in a commercial era.

In February 1993, this recommendation was leaked to the *South Wales Echo* and the end result was a no confidence vote in the union's general committee and Pugh himself becoming the union chairman. Then from 1994–95, he served as the IRB chairman for the statutory one-year term of office to be succeeded by Frenchman Bernard Lapasset when rugby was declared an open sport. In 1996 he returned as the IRB's first elected chairman and retained the post for two consecutive three-year terms. With a new era with players being paid, he became a driving force behind the expansion of the sport's World Cup and the Heineken Cup, the replacement of the old National Stadium with the much-admired Millennium Stadium in Cardiff and the realisation that Sevens' inclusion as an Olympic sport was a route to attracting newcomers to rugby union.

Pugh was not without his enemies. New Zealand RFU chairman Murray McCaw dismissed him as "a town planning QC running a global sport" after the Welshman ended his country's original role as co-hosts of the 2003 World Cup during an acrimonious dispute over commercial issues.

In 2014 Spiro Zavos, the highly regarded New Zealand-born writer based in Australia, went far further, condemning Pugh as a Machiavellian administrator conspiring against the interests of the southern hemisphere countries. His listed misdeeds included trying unsuccessfully to get the 2003 World Cup switched to France and "thugging SANZAR countries to ensure referees in the Super Rugby competition officiated in the strictest application of the black letter of rugby's complex laws".

Zavos added dismissively: "Pugh made it clear in his emails to SANZAR that he was totally opposed to the continuity and entertaining rugby game that teams like the Brumbies and Crusaders were developing. Instead of the try-fest Super Rugby were delivering, Pugh insisted on a game that was dominated by set pieces and penalties."

This viewpoint was not shared by everyone, for many regarded Super Rugby with its high scores more like basketball than rugby. When New Zealand's Chiefs defeated the South African-based Lions 72–65 in a match in 2010, one was left wondering if this was really a rugby game, looking at the final score. Whatever Pugh's faults, there was something slightly bizarre about damning an administrator for insisting the laws of a sport should be enforced rigorously. It is worth remembering players are responsible for penalty-ridden matches, as penalties are solely awarded when players fail to abide by the laws of the sport, while scrums are the result of player errors.

More damningly, Zavos also related the story that Pugh, no longer alive to answer his critic, had "tried to have the Wallabies thrown out of the tournament" when the eventual winners played Wales during the 1999 World Cup, as he mistakenly thought the Australians had brought a player back onto the field illegally during their 24–9 victory.

The accusation proved unfounded as the player had left the field with a blood injury so was perfectly entitled to return to play after treatment. It also provided ammunition for those accusing the IRB chairman of favouring northern hemisphere rugby in general and Wales in particular.

Pugh was not a man to avoid confrontation but how long he could have continued his dominant role as the game's main administrator may have been debatable. Sadly, the professional era saw rugby sleepwalking its way into crisis mode through taking too many wrong turns after his untimely death.

One of the major problems was the damage done by IRB/ World Rugby being content to back referees ignoring some of their own laws. Some 14 years of players getting away with crooked scrum feeds ended a fundamental feature of the sport – the art of hooking. Pugh's attitude to lax refereeing in Super Rugby offered little doubt he would not have tolerated the end of the straight scrum feed. Just as he ended the hypocrisy of rugby remaining an amateur sport when leading southern hemisphere players were obviously being paid to play the game, it is hard to imagine with his legal background he would have allowed World Rugby to commit the equally grating hypocrisy of deceiving the public by getting referees to allow illegal scrum feeds and then ignoring the widespread condemnation that followed.

It is also difficult to imagine he would have tolerated referees not only ignoring certain laws to keep the play flowing but also frequently warning players verbally during play itself not to commit offences. As rugby columnist Colin Boag wrote in *The Rugby Paper* in 2019, "Why do referees feel the need to stop players infringing? The players should know all the laws and if they decide to break them that's their choice and they should have to accept the consequences."

In 2007, Dr Ken Quarrie, a leading rugby injuries specialist, and Will Hopkins, New Zealand RFU's injury prevention officer, published a revealing study of Bledisloe Cup matches involving New Zealand and Australia between 1972 and 2004. They found in 1995 matches were lasting 83.7 minutes and the average playing time for players starting the game was 79.4 minutes. By 2004 the situation had changed dramatically with players starting the match averaging 64.3 minutes on the field before being replaced. This indicated the impact player rather than the tactical replacement was arriving at the game's top level. Before long, rugby union became a 23-man sport, significantly changing the nature of the game in terms of physicality, complexity and coaching and player costs.

It was Pugh himself who announced to the world in 1996 that tactical replacements would be allowed for the first time in the game of rugby union when the subs bench was extended from four to six players. Five players were allowed as replacements who could take the field at any time but two of the five had to be front row forwards. Players could not return to play once they had been replaced unless they had been treated for a blood injury.

In theory, the law change may have appeared a sensible way of improving the game, for as Pugh stated: "By allowing substitutes, an opportunity is being provided to enhance team performance. We also believe this decision makes the game more honest in that it addresses concerns about players feigning injuries."

The reality was this law change backfired, wrecking the balance of the game with the later emergence of the eight-man subs bench laden with powerful impact players who could take the field and go flat out against tiring players who had started the game. It takes a strong character to admit they have made a mistake, but one would like to think this damaging escalation of physicality through allowing tactical subs would not have been tolerated by Vernon Pugh had he not died in 2003.

With the Covid-19 health crisis increasing rugby's problems and private equity firms prepared to offer vast sums for a stake in the game's future as rugby union neared the 25th anniversary of the game going open, Pugh's philosophy was more relevant than ever. As he had stated: "Professionalism brings problems. There is a danger of the ethos being polluted, and that is why we must have strong managers. We have to stand up to aggressive commercial concerns who want to put money solely in the pockets of the few."

In May 2020, Sir Bill Beaumont, the amiable former England and British & Irish Lions captain, was re-elected chairman of World Rugby at the age of 68 after defeating the former Argentinian captain Agustín Pichot, his 45-year-old rival, by 28 votes to 23. During his election campaign, with the virus crisis dramatically changing the world's sporting landscape, Beaumont promised his second term would be about "change, reform and ambition". But there had been little evidence of these qualities in his first four years as chairman, where his leadership of the sport was a world away from the decisive approach of Vernon Pugh and his claim that "player welfare" was his main priority bore little relation to reality.

Pugh and Beaumont had contrasting experiences as rugby players. The Welshman was a junior club centre unable to gain a regular place with a major club, while Beaumont was a talented lock forward and popular leader who succeeded at the game's top level. On 17 November 1979, he captained the North of England to a memorable 21–9 victory over the All Blacks at Otley, outscoring the tourists by four tries to one. Then in 1980, he led England to the country's first Grand Slam in the Five Nations since 1957 and later that year captained the British & Irish Lions tour to South Africa, where the tourists lost a close-fought series 3–1 and won all 14 fixtures outside the Tests.

As rugby administrators, the contrast between the two men was equally stark. While Pugh had the vision and decisiveness that marked a great administrator, by contrast Beaumont was reluctant to court conflict off the field. This was reflected in his somewhat uninspired attitude to change, and when campaigning for re-election he stated: "I like to think that throughout my rugby administration I have been able to reach consensus."

The potential folly of placing consensus above conviction was illustrated when Beaumont – obviously embarrassed – sheepishly announced that the World Rugby Council had voted to make France hosts of the 2023 World Cup, rejecting the 139-page independent report which had recommended

South Africa as hosts and been backed unanimously by the Rugby World Cup Limited board.

The conservatism hampering rugby's future was reflected in the fact that rugby nations with the talent to challenge to the supremacy of the game's major powers remained in relative limbo in 2020, no better off than they had been 25 years earlier. The professional years had seen the major nations taking advantage of the flimsy international qualification regulations to recruit the best players in the production line of outstanding talent produced by the Pacific Island nations, Fiji, Samoa and Tonga. The fact former Samoa star Daniel Leo, a forthright crusader championing the cause of islands rugby, was not recruited by World Rugby to help end the financial inequality facing these hugely gifted rugby countries looked like yet another lost opportunity as Beaumont's second term got under way.

Rugby union is far too complex a sport ever to match the appeal of soccer, the world's most popular game, in either spectator or commercial terms. The reality is the oval ball game will always be a world away from the fantasy financial world inhabited by soccer in which agent Mino Raiola reportedly earned £41 million for merely masterminding French international star Paul Pogba's £89 million transfer from Juventus to Manchester United in 2016.

But does this really matter? The fact an astonishing 54 million people, just over half Japan's population, watched their countrymen defeat Scotland in the 2019 World Cup, and the ability of Test rugby to fill stadiums throughout the world, with vast numbers of supporters crossing the equator to support the British & Irish Lions, showed the game of rugby union had enough appeal and was providing enough income for the unions, players and coaches, without surrendering control to the moneymen.

Reverse the law changes that created the injury crisis in the first place, and a wonderful future for the game beckoned as full advantage could be taken of World Rugby's impressive initiatives to spread the rugby gospel worldwide. But it was not to be in the sport's first 25 years of professionalism.

In his *Rugby Paper* column on 6 May 2018, Jeremy Guscott, the outstanding former England centre remembered for his silken running skills and the drop-kick that gave the Lions a series victory in South Africa in 1997, with commendable clarity voiced the route to a golden era for the game of rugby union in the 21st century. "We have to make the breakdown more competitive because the current application of the laws has made it so hard to win the ball from the attacking team. I want the game to be true to its heritage and refereed as it used to be. If we fix the breakdown, reduce substitutions and sort out the scrum, our game will be one hell of a spectacle."

The state of the sport on 27 August 2020, 25 years after the end of amateurism, hardly matched Vernon Pugh's vision for the future of the game. Fellow Welshman Sir Gareth Edwards, heralded by many as the greatest of all rugby union players, lamented the game had become "a cross between rugby league and American football". This may have been regarded as an exaggeration by many but there was no doubt it had become a vastly different game.

Rome was burning and nobody had shown the courage to put the fire out.

Also from Y Lolfa:

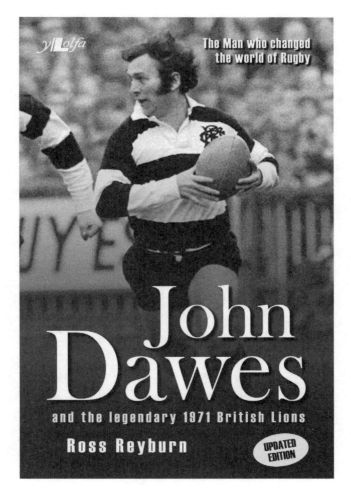

£9.99

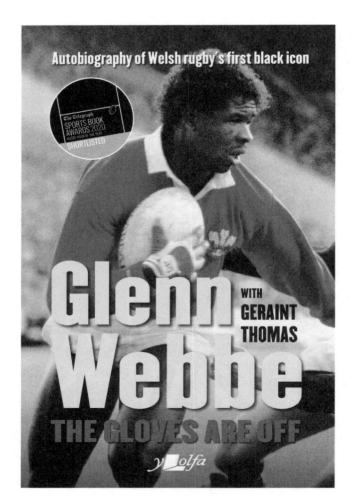

Autobiography of Welsh rugby's first black icon

The Telegraph
SPORTS BOOK
AWARDS 2020
RUGBY BOOK OF THE YEAR
SHORTLISTED

# Glenn Webbe

WITH
GERAINT
THOMAS

## THE GLOVES ARE OFF

y Lolfa

£9.99